70 Years Next To

Paradise

Water falls near Eutsuk Lake.

By ALAN BLACKWELL

Printed in Canada

2nd Printing, 1999

Book design by Power Line Productions of Burns Lake.
Editing, typesetting, and layout by Michael Turkki.
Cover photography of Eutsuk Lake by Alan Blackwell.

Canadian Cataloguing in Publication Data

Blackwell, Alan., 1923-
   70 Years Next To Paradise

   ISBN 1-55056-590-7

   1. Blackwell, Alan, 1923- 2. History - British Columbia

Peter & Gabby Braakkens

July 4/04

To Peter & Gabby with best wishes

This Book is dedicated to My Family and Friends.

Alan Blackwell

FOREWORD

*"At the gates of the forest ... is sanctity which shames our religions, and
reality that discredits our heroes. Here we find Nature to be the circumstance which dwarfs every other circumstance, and judges like a god all
men that come to her."*

This eloquent passage, written more than a century ago by Ralph
Waldo Emerson, has always been a favourite of mine -- perhaps as
much for its simplicity as its brilliance. In a mere fifty words, the man
many consider America's greatest philosopher described with rare clar-
ity nature's message and the joyful impact it can have upon a receptive
soul.

I don't know if Alan Blackwell ever read Emerson's essay entitled
Nature, but having worked closely with him to produce *Seventy Years
Next To Paradise*, I suspect he would agree with the philosopher's
comments. After all, why else would a man whose travels exposed him
to some of mankind's greatest cultural achievements return time and
time again to Northern B.C. and a community whose sole claim to fame
might be its proximity to Tweedsmuir Park? Indeed, it seems likely that
in Emerson or Henry David Thoreau, Alan would find a kindred spirit;
surely, only an individual whose heart beats in time with nature's sub-
tle rhythms would abandon so readily the comforts of civilization for a
rough but rich life in the wilderness.

The book you are about to read, *Seventy Years Next To Paradise,* is
first and foremost an entertaining look at one man's extraordinary life.
Yet with its descriptions of pioneer life and the events that helped mold
the author's character, it accomplishes much more than the average autobiography. In fact, though perhaps as much by accident as design, it
also affords readers a rare glimpse into the social, cultural, and economic development of the Ootsa Lake area -- and for this reason, if no
other, should be read.

In closing, there is little doubt that Alan Blackwell has made an im-
mense contribution to his community over the years. By writing and
publishing *Seventy Years Next To Paradise,* however, he has made an
even greater and more personal one. For this I thank him.

Michael Turkki

CONTENTS

FOREWORD

1. CHAPTER 1 - The Pioneer Years   5

2. CHAPTER 2 - My Childhood & Teen Years   25

3. CHAPTER 3 - The Years of Army Training   35

4. CHAPTER 4 - Italy and Southern France   44

5. CHAPTER 5 - England   55

6. CHAPTER 6 - Back in Canada   64

7. CHAPTER 7 - Our Year in Vancouver   79

8. CHAPTER 8 - Back At Ootsa Lake and the Park   85

9. CHAPTER 9 - Guiding and Electrical   103

10. CHAPTER 10 - Travel   113

11. CHAPTER 11 - Our Years in Gold Mining   123

12. CHAPTER 12 - Forced Retirement   141

    Bibliography and Thanks   150

CHAPTER ONE
The Pioneer Years

My father, Ed Blackwell, was born May 8, 1878, in Duxford, England. He joined the navy at a young age, and rose to the rank of admiral's cook. He sailed the seas for several years.

After immigrating to Canada in the early 1900's, Dad joined the Mounted Police in Calgary, Alberta. He left there in approximately 1907 and came to B.C., where he ran boarding houses between Prince Rupert and Hazelton during the building of the railroad.

During the year 1909, Dad and friend Shorty Matheson hiked from Hazelton to Ootsa Lake and claimed two parcels of land. This place had a fantastic view overlooking the Ootsa Lake valley; I often heard my father say it was the most beautiful place he had ever seen.

After claiming their parcels of land in 1909, Dad and Shorty returned to the 'outside world.' However, the following year they came back to Ootsa Lake and started building on the properties. They erected a decently-sized log cabin on Dad's place and a smaller one on Shorty's. Two years later, when Shorty acquired another parcel of land four miles to the east, Dad took over the adjoining property; that same year, Dad's brother Allan Blackwell came out from England to join him. Together, the brothers built a barn on Dad's place and started a cabin on land that my Uncle Allan staked next to Dad.

Unfortunately, this cabin was never finished, as the First World War broke out in 1914. Like many young men of the era, my uncle Allan and neighbour Arthur Shelford enlisted. Sadly enough, Allan never returned; I am told he was killed in action at the Battle of Mons on the last day of hostilities.

Despite the loss of his brother, Dad continued to develop the farm, acquiring more land and cattle, and adding more buildings. In 1920, though, he proposed to Allan's fiancee, Maud Spicer, whom they had both known since childhood. I've heard it said that before leaving for the war, Allan asked Dad to look after Maud if he was killed.

The war years, and those immediately after, must have been difficult for the young woman who was to be my mother. My uncle Allan and Maud were to be married as soon as the war was over; in fact, I am told that she was working in London, England when word came through of his death, and had already chosen her wedding dress. Yet much to Dad's surprise, she accepted his proposal and agreed to come to Canada.

Mother sailed for Canada in late September 1921. She landed at Montreal, then traveled by train to Telkwa, B.C. She met Dad there, and they were married in the Anglican Church on Oct. 23, 1921. This old church still stands in Telkwa.

Their honeymoon was a trip by wagon from Houston to Ootsa Lake. Mother often spoke of this experience. It seems that on the first night, Dad made a spruce bough bed under a tree. In the middle of the night, there was a rustling under their bed. Mother jumped up, screaming: "What is that?"

"Go back to sleep," Dad answered calmly, "it's only a mouse."

The 'honeymoon' continued; it took them three days to get to the homestead. By that time, I am sure the log cabin was a welcome sight.

All this must have come as quite a shock to a lady from the middle of London. Indeed, Mother told me that she cried herself to sleep many nights. It's difficult to imagine how she must have felt under these strange circumstances.

For the next two years, Mother and Dad worked the farm, increased their herd of cattle, and fixed up the house. Dad also

ABOVE: My father, Ed Blackwell, cooking in camps during the 1940s.

LEFT: My uncle, Allan Blackwell, shortly before he was killed in 1918.

Lillian and Maud Spicer in London, circa 1918.

My parents, Ed and Maud Blackwell, at their Ootsa Lake property.

took mother to meet the neighbours.

Since the end of the war, a number of settlers had moved into the area. Jack and Arthur Shelford had both married English women, and the members of these families became life-long friends.

Our closest neighbours were the Mohr family, and they also became close friends. I will not name all the families in the valley, as there have been several books written on the history of this area. However, I will mention those families that we had the closest contact with, and those people who influenced or impressed me the most during the more than 70 years I have lived in the Ootsa Lake valley.

During the early days, folks had to manufacture their own entertainment. Surprise parties were often held on Saturday evenings. Families would get together, play games, sing and dance to music supplied by the area's many musicians. My father, I've heard, added spice to any party; he always had a joke to tell, and always laughed at his own jokes. I've often wondered if people thought his jokes were good, or laughed only because they thought it polite to do so.

Erland Larsen was one local resident who manufactured his own entertainment, though of the liquid variety. Erland, who married a sister to the Shelfords, was noted for his excellent rhubarb wine. He called it "rhubarb pop," and in the winter months, always carried a bottle or two in his sleigh. There were also some moonshiners in the area who were noted for their fine products, but I will not mention their names.

In any event, Erland (or perhaps his 'pop') was popular with some of his neighbours, my father being one them. Dad was not one to drink moonshine, but he did like a nip of brandy now and again -- and didn't mind sampling some of Erland's concoctions.

I remember one time when Dad rode with Erland Larsen to the post office. It being a cold day, they were sipping on Erland's 'pop', but must have 'sipped' a little too much, because when Dad arrived home, he wasn't feeling well. Thinking he had the 'flu, Mother made him go to bed, but asked him if there was anything he wanted. Knowing she had a bottle of brandy that was used for cooking, Dad said maybe a small drink would help. Being a good-hearted sort, Mother -- who generally never let Dad drink any of her cooking brandy -- gave him a glass of the spirit. She was very angry when she heard the true story behind Dad's 'illness', and realized that he'd conned her to get a drink.

Another family very much involved in the community of Wistaria were the Harrisons. The Harrisons were a large family, or -- to be more accurate -- a group of families, and they contributed to the area in many ways. They had the first sawmill; some of them farmed, others were trappers. I had many good times with the Harrison children, many of whom were close to my own age.

My sister, brother, and I attended school with the Harrison children. Many are still close friends, but after the flooding of Ootsa Lake by the Aluminum Company of Canada, most of them left Wistaria. However, we are now related to them, as Ron Harrison (Alford Harrison's son), is married to Nadine, our eldest daughter.

The Robert Nelson family had the local post office, which served as the community meeting place on mail days. The Nelsons were a great asset to the area, and their only daughter, Alice, married Alford Harrison.

I must also mention the Charlie Moore family. Like the Harrisons, the Moores had a sawmill and also ran a farm. As I recall, there were two Moore boys at home, and they liked to sit in the front room with their father and chew tobacco. For convenience's sake, they kept a spittoon in the middle of the floor; in all the times we visited, I never once saw one of them miss it.

I can't forget Mrs. Moore, either, as she served as midwife to my mother when I was born. She always teased me, saying that when she held me up on her hand, I left it full.

The Moores lived in the area for many years, and a granddaughter -- Laura Henson -- still lives here. She was Pearl Moore's daughter, and never married. Grandson Milt Moore (Art Moore's son) works for the B.C. Forest Service in Dease Lake, B.C., and he has children; in fact, last year (1997) we attended a wedding reception for Milt's son Les and our niece Lisa Palmer.

The Kerrs also lived at Wistaria in the early years. Bill Kerr, the local undertaker, had a brother who was killed during the First World War. Bill's brother had already married prior to his death, though, and he and Mrs. Kerr had three children: Doug, Mel, and Mary. The two boys moved away when I was young, but Mother visited Mrs. Kerr often. Mary Kerr eventually married Al Ford from Smithers and took up residence there. In later years, after Bill died, Mrs. Kerr also moved to Smithers. Mother continued to visit her there.

The Pete Kerr family included two children, Roy and Edna, and for a time we went to school with them. Roy and Edna later moved to Victoria, and I didn't see them again for decades. Then, while on a business trip to B.C.'s capital city in 1997, I had the opportunity to visit both of them. Roy is in a home for the elderly; he had a stroke a few years ago, but is doing well. Edna and her husband, meanwhile, are still quite spry. It was certainly a pleasure to see the Kerrs again after so many years.

Jim Nelson and family were well-known in Wistaria, and I visited them often. I really admired the Nelsons; Jim Sr. had such a great sense of humour, even though he suffered much pain. Stricken with arthritis, he passed away at an early age; he and his wife Bella, however, had two children, Minnie and Jim. I went to school with both. Jim Jr. never married, and died of a heart attack at a relatively young age. Minnie, meanwhile, married and had two children, Doug and Colleen. Minnie lost her husband when he was still a young man, but still lives at Wistaria -- as does her son Doug, now married with his own family. Colleen also married and resides in Fort Fraser.

Shorty Matheson, who I've already mentioned as having homesteaded with Dad, remained a neighbour. He lived with the Jim Nelson family for many years, and was their helper until his death.

My family also had some kin move into the area while I was still young. In 1927, Mother's cousin Mabel Talbot and her husband Fred came out from England. They stayed with us until they were able to find a place of their own. They bought a place at Streatham and lived there for many years, raising two children, Joy and Neville.

Fred and Mabel passed away some time ago; Joy, however,

married Ben Guenter, and the two took over the Talbot farm at Streatham, where they raised three children. They were good friends and neighbours to us for many years, but eventually sold their property to the Jessees and Stillers and moved to Smithers. Joy, now widowed, still lives there, but we see her often.

Sadly enough, Neville drowned in Ootsa Lake when he was a young man. Despite this fact, he remains very much alive in my memory -- for one incident in particular.

I was taking correspondence at Streatham school the year Neville started there, and (like yours truly) he still had a broad English accent at the time of enrollment. I recall that shortly after his arrival at school, he had occasion to visit the outhouse. Neville didn't stay long, though; in fact, within a few minutes of his departure from class, the door flew open and there he stood with his pants down around his ankles.

"I'm not going in there," Neville said with his strong English accent, "there's a mole mouse in there."

As might be expected, everyone laughed. "Alan," the teacher said to me, "please go and help him." I graciously did, and I'm sure Neville was thankful for my assistance at the time. However, he didn't appreciate being teased about this incident when he was older.

A short while after the Talbots moved into the area, Fred Spicer came to live with us. For many years, my sister, brother, and I thought he was our uncle, but later learned he was our half-brother. I suppose the truth was kept from us for a reason, but it was unfortunate, as it caused problems for both Fred and his family.

I learned of this 'skeleton' in the family closet during the Second World War, but as I promised, never told anyone until after Mother passed away. When I told my brother and sister, we all agreed that it was sad that the truth had not come out many years before. One thing that bothered me was the fact that although Fred's children had the same grandmother as mine, they were unable to call Mother "Grandma."

Yet Fred was a true brother to me; he taught me how to swim and was very patient. He also taught me how to dance, which

Our dog on Tweedsmuir Mountain in the park.

Dad's car, the Willys Whippet, and some envious young folks.

A group of young people at Wistaria during the early years of the war. (Pictured here are: Hugh Shelford, Myles Shelford, John Anderson, Peggy Shelford, John Shelford, Pat Carroll, Charles Priest, Alma Anderson, Phyllis Harrison, Lucille Harrison, me, Babs Barker, Millie Blackwell, Alice Nelson.)

proved a great asset in my social life; in fact, if truth be known, he was a big influence on my whole life. Fred, now 89 years old, lives alone and still leads an active life. His wife Molly passed away several years ago; they had two boys, Anthony (who is married with a family and lives in Prince George) and Norman (who, along with his wife Verla, lives in Burns Lake). At the time of my writing this book, Fred, Anthony, and the latter's wife had just returned from a trip to England, where they were visiting relatives.

Being older than I, Fred was around to witness much of my early childhood. I was talking with him the other day, and he told me that when I was seven years old, I went for a walk in the pasture and got lost. He said I was bawling like crazy, so he came to rescue me. As it turned out, I was only a few hundred yards from the house, and about 20 yards off the trail. The story seems testament to a poor sense of direction on my part; had the hunters I guided later in life heard it, I'm sure they would have been more than a little nervous.

Fred was an integral part of our family, and perhaps the best driver of the lot. In approximately 1931, Dad bought a 1929 Willys Overland Whippet. The car was a real lemon, and Fred had to do the driving, because Dad couldn't seem to master it.

One day, Fred was trying to teach Dad to drive; they went to a large, flat area beyond the barn. Dad got behind the wheel, put the Whippet in gear, and away they went.

"Take your foot off the gas, Ed," Fred yelled, but Dad just kept shouting: "Whoa, whoa, whoa." One thing led to another, and they ended up on a rock pile in the bottom of a gully. It took a team of horses to pull the car out, and Dad never again tried to drive.

During my years of growing up, I had many good friends, the closest being the four Shelford boys: John, Hugh, Myles, and Cyril. They spent a lot of time trapping, and also shot a lot of squirrels with a .22 calibre rifle. I've been told that most of those squirrels were shot in the head, but I also know the Shelford boys missed occasionally -- and when they did, it often led to quite a show.

The Shelfords were allowed one shell per squirrel, so if they missed, they had to get it by other means. I lived four miles away, and on a clear day, I knew by the noise when they were getting a squirrel by 'other means.' Two of the boys would climb the trees, while the other two -- armed with clubs -- stayed on the ground. The two in the trees made a lot noise in an effort to flush the squirrel out, and on occasion, even resorted to jumping from one tree to another. I'm sure sometimes the squirrel died of fright. I don't know if the Shelfords ever lost an animal, but I do know they sold enough squirrel skins to buy a Model A Ford truck.

We had many good times together. The four Shelford boys took their schooling, Grade One through Eight, by correspondence, so they never lost their English accent completely. Cyril is the only one of the four still alive, and retired to Victoria after spending several years in politics (including some as provincial Minister of Agriculture). He's also the author of several books -- *From Snowshoes To Politics, We Pioneered, Think Wood,* and *From War to Wilderness* -- and all are worth reading.

Cyril and I went through the war in Italy, but did not see each other until on leave in England near the end of hostilities.

I'll always remember the marital advice given us by the boys' father, Jack Shelford. "When you meet a girl that you plan to marry," he said, "take a good survey of her mother, because it's likely the daughter will be like her mother."

Before the war, the Shelfords had a log raft that we used for fishing on Eastern Lake. Cyril would tie a line on his toe, swim around until he caught a fish, then climb back on the raft and retrieve it. Some folks hesitate to believe this, but I have seen him catch quite a few fish with his toe line.

All four boys were good at throwing rocks, too, and proved particularly adept at hitting grouse in the head. Their prowess with stones sometimes landed them in hot water, though.

One day, when they were picking potatoes with their bald-headed Uncle Arthur, Hugh bet Myles that he could not hit the elder man on the head with a potato. Myles took the challenge. Arthur, bent over and concentrating on the work, was coming down the next row about fifty feet away; Myles nailed him dead in the center of his bald head. The spud splattered, Arthur yelled: "Myles!", and the race was on.

As expected, Arthur won. Myles got a real ass-warming. It was incredible that Myles was blamed, because Arthur never even looked up before he yelled. Hugh laughed for the rest of the day. He knew that Myles, the group's prankster, would be blamed.

As you can tell, the Shelfords were real characters. I remember one incident before the war, when a group of us was having a swimming party at Eastern Lake about a mile from the Shelfords' property. Mary Ford, a local girl then married and living in Smithers, brought some friends to visit. One of the visitors was a beautiful redhead who seemed to like John Shelford, and had been flirting a little with him. John, however, was very shy and embarrassed easily.

As the party got underway, the girls retired to a big spruce tree back in the bush, where they proceeded to change into swimsuits. After they abandoned this primitive change room in favour of a dip in Eastern Lake, Cyril and I nonchalantly tied their clothes in knots -- then waited for the commotion to start.

After their swim, the bathing beauties exited the water and went to change. A few minutes later, the pretty red-headed girl came bursting out of the woods with nothing on but her panties. Blaming John, she ran right up to him and said: "Little Napoleon, you tied these up, you untie them." John took one look at her, gasped, and headed off through the woods like a moose going for water. He was blamed for the knots; Cyril and I took our time undoing them and enjoying the scenery.

The rest of the boys were not as shy as John, especially Cyril. I will not tell of the capers he and I participated in while on leave in England during the war.

In addition to the Shelfords, as a youngster I spent a great deal of time with the Loren Priest family. Loren and his wife have been gone for many years, but I shall always remember them; they were like second parents to me. In fact, I consider the entire Priest family as one of my favourites.

Molly, the eldest Priest girl, married my half-brother Fred. She had been married previously and divorced. Polly Priest was married to Norm Pratt; they operated a store in the area in later years. Maude, Polly's sister, married Orald Harrison, and they lived at

Wistaria until Alcan flooded Ootsa Lake. Later, Maude and Orald moved to Salmon Arm; they eventually separated, and both re-married. Maude now lives in Quesnel, and Orald on Vancouver Island. Audrey Priest, meanwhile, left here and went to Tofino, where Norm and Polly lived at that time. She still lives on Vancouver Island, but visits this area every summer. She lost her first husband to cancer, but has a large family, all of whom reside on the Island.

Stewart, the eldest Priest boy, lived here for a long time but later moved south. He passed away in Quesnel two years ago.

Over the years, I have kept in touch with all the Priests, yet it is perhaps Loren's son Charles whom I was closest to in the early years. We worked, trapped, and had fun together for many years. Charles, his wife Doris, and most of their family still live here, and have one of the largest cattle ranches in the area. Their eldest son Alan works with his father, and now has a large family of his own. All of them are hard workers, and contribute greatly to the success of the ranch. Several of Alan's beautiful daughters will soon make excellent wives for a few lucky boys.

The tiny community of Streatham also included the Olaf Anderson family (Olaf and children John, Doris, and Alma). Mrs. Anderson had passed away earlier, but I always enjoyed visiting with Olaf; he had many interesting stories of the early days.

I recall one story in particular. According to Olaf, one settler had been dating a girl in some small town and was coming very close to popping the question. However, his neighbour had also taken a fancy to this same gal, and pulled a real dirty trick.

The neighbour, after considerable conniving, rounded up a native girl who was "selling her services" and spent the night with her. In the morning, he apologized for not having any money to complete the transaction, but said he'd left it with friends in town. The neighbour then gave the name of the unsuspecting victim's girlfriend. Needless to say, the welcome the victim received on his next visit to his beloved was not what he expected.

I've heard that years later, after the prankster had passed away, someone told the unwitting victim what had happened. Upon learning the truth, the man in question jumped off his seat and yelled: "It's a damn good thing that bastard is dead, or I would go and kill him right now."

In addition to anecdotes like the above, I also heard a great deal of this area's history from Olaf. He came in to the Ootsa Lake country over the Bella Coola trail, and knew all the original settlers.

After World War Two, Alma Anderson married G. Addison, known to everyone as 'Chuck.' They have lived here ever since and worked the Anderson ranch. They have toiled hard and -- in addition to being wonderful friends and neighbours -- been very successful. Alma and Chuck have one daughter, Heather, who is married and lives in Smithers.

Heather was a good friend of our daughter Nadine, and I have some good movies of them playing together. Heather is quite a comedian and at times embarrassed her mother. She comes by it naturally, though, because her father can be quite a clown at times. It is always a pleasure to see Heather and share her sense of humour.

No story about the Ootsa Lake valley would be complete without mention of the Schriebers, who lived at Ootsa Lake. Norman Schrieber, the area's mail-carrier, would pick parcels and letters up on the north side of Francois Lake and deliver them to all the post offices to the south, the last one being at Wistaria.

Norman, originally from Ontario, came to the Ootsa Lake area after serving in the First World War. After moving here, he married Ootsa Lake school teacher Grace Graham. The Schriebers opened a general store in 1932, and it remained in operation until 1946. Their son Dick served in the Second World War, and after returning to this area, operated a trucking business. Dick and I eventually became brothers-in-law, as we both married Anderson girls (whose parents had originally settled at Danskin, five miles south of the Francois Lake ferry).

Dick Schrieber and I were very good friends; we flew a lot together, as Dick had a small plane. Later, while working for Omineca Air Services (owned by Bill Harrison Jr. of Wistaria), he flew hunters and supplies for my business, Tweedsmuir Park Guides and Outfitters. Tragedy ended Dick's career; he was killed in a plane accident at Stewart, B.C. in 1960. The Schriebers' daughter, Anne -- who became a nurse -- is married with a family and still lives in Burns Lake.

The Schriebers sold their store at Ootsa Lake in 1946 to Art Pelletier and his wife Polly. Formerly a Harrison, she became a school teacher and married Art at Jasper, Alberta. The couple spent their early years together in the Peace River area, and were a real asset to the Ootsa Lake community upon their arrival here. After the flooding, the Pelletiers lived in Vancouver for a while, where my wife Marion and I (during our brief stint as city-dwellers) had the pleasure of having them as close friends. Though Marion and I only tolerated life in Vancouver for one year, the Pelletiers remained. They eventually moved to Prince George, though, where they operated a store. Art died there in 1985; Polly spent the last years of her life in a Prince George nursing home. Their son Stan still lives in P.G., while another son, Alfred, lives in Williams Lake.

The Pratt family came to Ootsa Lake in 1948 from Tofino on Vancouver Island, and Norm Pratt and Orald Harrison each bought a quarter share in Pelletiers' store. Norm Pratt was married to Polly Priest, and they had two children: Patti and Duff. After the flooding, the Pratts sold and moved to Clearwater, B.C. Norm passed away in 1961. Polly remarried after his death, but I heard recently that she died in Kamloops Hospital at the age of 85. I visited her last May and am happy I did. She was one of my favourite people.

The Van Tines have also been permanent fixtures at Ootsa Lake. Members of a large family, they are scattered over the province. Jim and his wife Arleen still carry on the guiding business started by his father. The Van Tines worked diligently over the years and have a successful business. I give credit to Arleen, who always has a smile and a cup of kindness for every-one.

Jim, a renowned story-teller, is adept at entertaining his clients. Whenever I get in a blue mood, I drop in to hear one of his dramatic stories. At one time or another, Jim must have insulted a grizzly, because two years in a row, these animals have wrecked his guiding camp on Eutsuk Lake. I understand this has cost him thousands of dollars. Perhaps, as I heard Paddy Carroll once say, he should go grizzly hunting. Jim's well-equipped for that, too; if the truth be known, he's big enough to hunt grizzly with a switch.

Merle Van Tine was killed in the Second World War, and Chuck was badly wounded. I spent a leave with Chuck in England in 1945, and am sorry to say he passed away in recent years.

Two other Wistaria residents who greatly impressed me were Paddy and Beatrice Carroll. Like Jim Van Tine, Paddy was a great story-teller and had a terrific sense of humour. I always enjoyed the Carrolls. When I was young, I also liked being around their daughters, Pat and Cecille.

Once, I asked Pat to go to a dance with me and she agreed. Being a decent sort, when Myles Shelford asked her shortly there after, she politely informed him she was already spoken for. Unfortunately for me, Myles laughed and told her: "Alan only asks you when other girls aren't available." I went to pick her up, but didn't go to the dance. I was busy nursing a black eye.

I remember a party at the Wistaria Hall. Paddy and his family had walked from Harrison Bay and were really having a good time. When the family was ready to go home, though, Paddy wouldn't budge; he wanted to stay for a few more drinks. His wife Beatrice (whom we always called 'Sammy') wasn't about to take any guff; uttering "No way," she grabbed his tie. Daughters Pat and Cecille pushed, and Paddy was on his way home.

On the trail back to Harrison Bay there was an old washed-out bridge; at the time, the creek under it was spanned only by a twelve-inch square timber. It was here that Sammy and the girls let Paddy loose. I'm sure they thought he'd fall in and sober up, yet much to their amazement, he backed up, took a run at the timber, and made the other side.

Turning to his family and laughing like hell, Paddy gleefully asked: "You thought I'd fall in, didn't you, Mother?" He walked the rest of the way home without assistance.

Jacob Lund is another pioneer who will always remain in my memory. He was a wonderful fellow, but as I remember, he always did things the hard way.

A case in point is the story involving Jacob and an unidentified old-timer. It seems they were packing gasoline across the Whitesail-Eutsuk portage, and the old-timer tied a 45-gallon drum of the fuel upright on a pack board, heaved it aloft, and took off with it. Not to be outdone, Jacob tied a drum on horizontally and carried it across the portage. If the story is true, the sloshing gasoline in its unwieldy container probably caused Jacob to travel twice the distance from side to side.

Jacob, a good friend and neighbour, commanded respect. Fred Spicer and I spent a winter logging with him; he was very strong, and on several occasions I saw him carry logs on his shoulders rather than hook a horse to them. It was an impressive feat, but being slightly lazy myself, I think I could have made work a little easier. He passed away some time ago.

There were, of course, many others who earned a place in my memory. The Rist family, for example, lived at Streatham. Bill Rist was the first postmaster, and he married Olaf Anderson's sister-in-law. The Rists had two children, Monica (who married Elmer Mohr) and Jessie (who spent her adult life in the southern part of the province). Billy died at an early age, so I do not remember him very well. However, the rest of the family were good friends. Mrs. Rist gave me a real talking-to when I was sixteen years old. It seems she didn't like me kissing her daughter, even though (as I recall) Jessie didn't seem to mind. We joked about it in later years.

During my early teens, a family moved on to a farm at the west end of Francois Lake. Their name was Grainger; they had four children: Martin, Barry, Kathleen, and Barbara. They became good friends and remained so. Of course, the parents have been gone for many years, and Barry joined them in the Here After some time ago. Martin and Kathleen both moved away from the area, and I recently heard that Martin passed away in the Vander-hoof hospital after suffering the effects of a stroke for some time.

I still see Barbara often, though. She and her husband live on the original Grainger homestead. Barb and I remain close. I remember her mother as being an exceptional pianist. I loved to sit and listen to her play.

Over the years, we spent many happy hours with members of the Grainger family. In fact, in the seventeen years I lived at Wistaria before I went to the army, I certainly had a good life; thinking back, I don't think we could have had better neighbours and friends.

Even during the Great Depression, there wasn't a time we went hungry. Aside from berries in the summer, we didn't have much fresh fruit, but we ate a lot of raw vegetables. Raw peeled potatoes with a little salt were delicious, as were raw turnips and cabbage. One boy brought raw turnips to school for lunch. Some kids today think we were nuts, and I sometimes wonder myself. Yet I have asked many people my age and most say that raw potatoes were a favourite treat.

Though people today might think ours was a boring life, nothing could be farther from the truth. We found plenty to occupy our time. We played a lot of baseball (the Harrisons, for example, were avid ball players), and during our teen years, attended many dances and parties. In addition to being a regular at local soirees, I rode 16 miles on horseback to dances at Tatalrose, stayed overnight with friends, then rode home the following day. I also went to dances at Colleymount and had good friends there, especially Hugh, Tom, and Margaret Cowan.

Many of the families, especially those of English extraction, belonged to the Anglican Church. However, because there wasn't a church in the area in the early years, we met once a month at different homes for church services. This was a social affair as well as a time of worship; we had dinner, organized games, and played cards in the afternoon. We always looked forward to these fun days.

I often think of the experiences we had. One weekend when I was fourteen years old, I took my brother Stan with me hunting for cows. We had our dog Gip with us.

About two miles from home, we ran into a bear with two cubs. The cubs went up a tree, and the mother bear came after Stan and I.

Fortunately, Gip came to our defense and went after the mother bear, which bought us a little more time. Stan started climbing a tree, but when I looked back, I couldn't believe my eyes.

My brother was climbing the same tree as the cubs.

I started yelling when Stan was eight feet or so up the tree. Realizing his mistake, he dropped from the tree like a ripe apple, and his legs were moving full speed when he hit the ground. We both took off at a speedy run and never looked back for a mile. Then we began to worry about the dog, but Gip caught up with us a little later. The mutt never even suffered a scratch.

I was thankful that we had such a trustworthy dog with us, but from that day on, I always carried a rifle.

About a year after the bear incident, a moose showed up in our field. As we were out of meat at the time, I took up the rifle, eager to shoot my first moose.

Things didn't go exactly according to plan, however. After I got within shooting distance of the moose, I looked back towards the barn where Fred Spicer was working with a team of horses. I must have had my finger on the trigger as I pumped a shell into the firing chamber, because the gun went off and killed Dad's favourite milk cow. Needless to say, my carelessness created a great deal of unhappiness in our household, and resulted in the cancellation of my gun-carrying privileges for a while.

Dad forgave me later, saying it was lucky I hit the cow instead of Fred.

Discipline around our home was strict when I was young, but we were spanked only when we did something truly bad. Being a bit of a hellion, I endured several spankings.

I always thought my sister Millie got away with things because she was a girl. However, I do remember one spanking she received.

Money was tight, and my parents had just bought me a set of suspenders to wear to school. (All boys had to wear suspenders in those days, particularly those from proper English families.) Well, Millie and I were having a little spat, and she took my yet-to-be-worn suspenders and put them in the slop pail. To say Mother and Father were a little annoyed when they found this out would be an understatement; to this day, I don't think Millie has forgotten the spanking she received.

I don't remember Stan getting spanked, but he was the youngest; Millie and I figured he was the pet. I left home when he was still young, though, and I heard he sampled the sting of the old man's strap a few times while I was away.

I left home in early spring 1941 after a disagreement with my father. Dad and I did not get along well during my teenage years, but when I returned from the war, I could not believe how much he'd changed while I was away. I'm sure many people realize how stupid they were as teenagers. As children, we often resented the punishment handed out by our parents; now, of course, we know they were merely trying to build good character and instill in us the values we'd need as adults.

I wonder how many people have thought about their childhood and the frustrations they caused their parents. For my part, I'm sure I could have been a much better son.

CHAPTER TWO
My Childhood and Teen Years

When I was born in my parents' Wistaria home on July 27, 1923, there were no doctors in the area. My mother was attended by Mrs. Charles Moore, a local midwife who assisted with many births. Premature, lacking fingernails and toenails, I weighed less than six pounds when born. A considerate friend of the family promptly informed Mother she should be prepared for the worst; I could not live for more than a few weeks, the friend said, and if I did, I would be a shrimp or an idiot. Well, while possibly an idiot, I am hardly a shrimp; at last weigh-in I tipped the scales at two hundred and twenty pounds. I have also lived slightly longer than the anticipated few weeks, reaching the ripe age of seventy-four in 1997.

I'm not sure how my parents felt about my arrival. Dad always told me that when born, I was so ugly that he turned me over three times before he could tell one end from the other.

I wasn't to be an only child, though. On March 29, 1926, my sister Millie was born, and on April 9, 1928, my brother Stanley came into the world. Both Dad and Mother were up in years when they raised their family.

As children, we had a great time at home. We traveled miles by wagon to visit friends, and we also had a lot of friends visit us. We had horses to ride and wonderful scenery to admire. There was a hill at the back of our place; we would ride up the hill or

That's me at an early age.

sometimes walk up just to admire the view. From there, we could see most of Ootsa Lake and the rugged mountains that later became part of Tweedsmuir Park. (This park is paradise to me, and is where I spent a lot of time in later years. Indeed, it was the scenery that prompted me to write this book and name it *Seventy Years Next To Paradise*. There will be more on the park later.)

When it came time for the children of Edgar and Maud Blackwell to attend school, plans had to be made. We lived four miles from school -- a distance too great for 'yours truly' to travel alone -- so my parents had me stay with the Mohr family. I walked to school with the Mohrs' offspring, Francis and Kathryn.

School was an entirely new experience for me, and not one that I greatly enjoyed. At the time, I spoke with a heavy English accent, and was the only child in the school who did. The Mohrs, meanwhile, were from the United States; consequently, the older boys made fun of everything I said. I hated every kid in school, and my parents had a difficult time keeping me there during the first few months.

Aside from Mother and Dad, the only person who kept me in class was my teacher, Dorothy Howe. I remember her as being tall and pretty, and so nice. Now in her mid-eighties, she lives in the Okanagan; I correspond with her occasionally, and recently received a photo of her. She told me she was only nineteen when she taught me Grade One in 1929. I was the only first grade student in the class that year.

I did have another ally in school, though. Miss Howe boarded with the Bob Nelson family, which included a daughter named Alice who happened to be a few years older than I. Alice protected me from the bullies in the school, and has been a close friend ever since. She's now almost family, too, as her son married my eldest daughter.

Although Grade One was a bit of a trial for me, my second year in school proved more pleasant. By that time, I had lost most of my broad accent and had made a few good friends.

My second grade teacher was Lulu Morgan, who in fact taught me for the next couple of years. Miss Morgan had grown up in the area; in fact, she was the first white baby born in the Ootsa Lake valley. Though not a very large girl when she taught at our school, I distinctly remember she could hit very hard with the strap.

The first morning of school after Easter, Miss Morgan told us she'd been married during the holidays. Her name, she stated firmly, was now Mrs. Beaver, and we were no longer to call her Miss Morgan. "If you can't think of my name," she added, "think of a long-tailed animal that swims in the lake."

I couldn't let this pass. After a while, I put up my hand and said quite seriously: "Mrs. Muskrat -- I mean, Mrs. Beaver!"

Well, that did it; the whole class started laughing, and I felt pretty smart. Unfortunately, Mrs. Beaver didn't share my sense of humour, and sentenced me to a noon hour at the blackboard, where I was forced to write "I must always treat my teacher with respect" five hundred times. That's a lot of writing for anyone, let alone a youngster, and I'll always remember it.

My sister Millie started school when Mrs. Beaver was teaching. Lulu, as we were able to call her later in life, was very good to all her students. She even loaned my family a horse, which enabled me to move back home and ride to school each morning. By this time, although the Mohrs were good to me and remained friends, I had stayed with them long enough.

Lulu stayed in the area for many years and taught in several schools; she and her husband Ab also raised a family and operated a country store. Lulu died a short time ago, having been predeceased by her beloved husband. We were saddened by their passing; they were good friends to us.

Prior to her marriage, Lulu boarded with the Cliff Harrison family; in fact, I recently learned that Mrs. Harrison designed and made Lulu's wedding dress. The Harrisons happened to be friends of my parents, and over the years, the Harrison children -- Bill, Marie, and Montie -- have themselves become good friends. Montie and my son Reg played in a dance band together for several years, though I regret to say that Montie passed away suddenly two years ago.

Marie Harrison, meanwhile, was only eleven when I entered the army, yet wrote me often during the five years I was away at war. I certainly appreciated her letters, and she has remained one of my favourite people. Bill has always been a friend, and we love his wife Rosemary. He's also been close to my brother Stan.

After Mrs. Beaver, my next teacher was Stella Pahkala. Like Miss Howe before her, she boarded with the Nelsons, and everyone liked her. My brother Stanley started school the year Miss Pahkala arrived, and he loved school from then on. She always maintained discipline in the school but rarely raised her voice. Stella passed away some time ago, but Alice has kept in contact with the family and they are sending her a memoir of Stella's first school in Boston Bar.

I attended Wistaria school until I graduated from Grade Eight. I had several teachers; I liked them all, but they never left the impression the first three did.

I mentioned earlier that I took schooling by correspondence.

This was tough for me. I was enrolled at the Streatham school this time; the Grade Nine correspondence class consisted of four girls and myself. My classmates did well that year, but I hated every minute of it. However, I did like our teacher; her name was Marjorie Westwood, and she assisted the five of us with our studies. She was only a few years older than her students, but we liked her. She was a very good teacher, and with her help, I managed to complete Grade Nine.

During this time, I again stayed with the Mohrs, who by now had moved to Streatham. I walked to school with Birdie (Kathryn) Mohr, but we did not like each other. We walked a hundred feet apart to and from school. I saw Birdie's husband and daughter last summer and was saddened to hear that Birdie's memory is gone and she does not know her family.

In the summer months, I helped Dad and Fred with the haying. During the summer of my sixteenth year, I had one of those embarrassing experiences no one really likes to remember but can never seem to forget.

Harold and Irene Roemer lived at Richardson Lake, about three miles away, so Irene often rode horseback to visit Mother. It was a very hot day when we came in for lunch; Irene was visiting. I sat down across the room from her and was shocked to find my jeans had split from front to back. I never wore underwear when it was hot, so you might say I was 'well exposed' -- not only to the elements, but the gaze of anyone within fifty feet. At sixteen, what could be more embarrassing? It is strange that in later years, Mrs. Roemer and I became related, as I married her niece. I have never mentioned the bare ass incident, and will probably regret doing so herein.

The following fall, I enrolled in the toughest school of all -- The School of Hard Knocks. First I tried trapping. A good friend, Charles Priest, and I trapped and cut firewood. We cut this wood for an old Dutch fellow who built a large log house on Ootsa. (This was before the flooding.) He was a tough man to work for, but we filled the contract. Yet there were times when we had to use some forceful negotiations.

In April, we started trapping muskrats. We had very good luck, but spent some cold days and nights.

It was during this time that both Charles and I came down with chicken pox. Itchy and miserable, we walked to Charles' sister's house. She was pregnant and had one young child at the time; she took one quick look at us, and shut the door in our faces. "Get out of here," she yelled. "I don't want to get chicken pox when I'm pregnant, and I don't want my young child to get chicken pox, either." We then walked another one and a half miles to Charles' parents' house, where we were very sick for a few days.

Trapping wasn't easy, but we had one consolation: When we had received the returns from our furs, we had more money than either of our parents.

Then again, there was never a lot of money around in those days. To make ends meet, Dad cooked in several road and relief camps during hard times. This was the only place to earn a few extra dollars, unless one could make railway ties with a broad axe (which is how Loren Priest made his extra dollars).

When I was in my teens, Dad was cooking in a road camp at Decker Lake. The foreman and Dad didn't like each other, so many strange things happened.

Jordy, the foreman, was always spying on Dad, trying to get something on him. Dad knew what was going on, though, and led his supervisor on a merry chase. Every night, Jordy would check the groceries and supplies, then figure up what had been used. He thought Dad was caching groceries to take home. Dad knew this, so he would move canned goods from one place to the other so it was difficult for Jordy to keep track of things.

One time, when Dad knew he was getting a week off starting the following Monday, he began digging a hole behind the cook tent. He made sure Jordy saw it and then dug a little each day until Friday arrived. When all the men were away on Friday, Dad took a big poop in the hole and covered it with a piece of cardboard upon which he'd inscribed: "Is this what you are looking for, Jordy?" He then filled the hole with dirt.

On Saturday, Jordy got a couple of men and started digging. That miserable man thought for sure he'd found a cache of groceries. Imagine Jordy's surprise when he found the groceries had already been digested.

Dad waited until Monday at breakfast, then said: "Nice pile of groceries in that hole, wasn't there, Jordy?"

All the men laughed, and that did it. Jordy jumped up and took a swing at Dad, which was not a wise thing to do. Dad had a bad temper and was angry by this time; he slapped that foreman in the face with an apple pie, threw him on the floor, and held him there with a knee in the stomach. Jordy didn't dig up any piles for a few days; he had two broken ribs. Dad came home for a week, and when he went back he was treated with respect. All the men in camp liked him as he was an excellent cook. The trick he pulled on Jordy was the laugh of the year.

Once Charles Priest and I became working stiffs, it wasn't long before we began to have a few strange experiences with employers. On one occasion, while Charles and I were doing a few days' work for a resident of the community, two ladies came by pulling a sleigh. "I don't want to involve you boys," the elder lady said, "but would you tell your boss that two ladies have gone behind his property pulling a sleigh?"

At the time, we didn't know what was going on. The fellow we were working for was a foreigner and new to the area. From what I could gather, it seems he owed the one of the ladies' husbands for working on his house, and there was a dispute over the amount.

When we found our employer, Charles and I told him where the ladies had gone. "Oh, mine Godt!" he exclaimed. "I shot a moose back there and I don't have a licence. I've got to stop them or I will lose mine guns." He then came to where we were working and waited until the two women came back dragging a moose head on their sleigh.

We kept working, but we could see that heated negotiations were underway. After some time, we saw our boss scratching out a cheque. The ladies dropped off the moose head, and with big smiles on their faces, went on home with the empty sleigh and a cheque.

As they were walking away, our boss pointed to them and said: "There are two ruthless women." We learned later that they wouldn't settle for a cent less than the amount they figured he owed the husband. In those days, we didn't need a lawyer to obtain fair settlement.

Whenever two people work together for a long time, they are bound to have disagreements. Charles and I had our share, but they were mostly over girls. It seemed we were always interested in the same girl. Unfortunately, Charles always won the girl over, probably because he had better lines than I.

During my teen years, I used to go to town once in a while, and always stopped to visit Fred and Jesse Coombes. Although we did not agree on politics or religion, they remained friends for their lifetimes. I called them Mark and Luke; this annoyed them, as they did not believe in the Bible. I took advantage of this 'soft underbelly', jokingly suggesting that some day, an evangelist would convert them and they'd both become crusaders who traveled the world thumping the Bible. Of course, this never happened, and they are both gone now, but they were great friends and a big help to all who needed assistance. When I wrote an exam for my Class B electrical ticket, I learned more from Jesse Coombes than all the books I could find on the subject.

By this time, it was 1940 and the Second World War was on. Fred Spicer, Scotty McIvor, and two of the Shelford boys -- Hugh and Cyril -- joined the artillery and were stationed in Prince Rupert. John Shelford joined the navy. It seemed everyone I knew was leaving.

Even though I was under-age, I went to town and tried to join. Someone squealed on me, though -- probably my parents. I was upset at the time, but later realized that Dad lost two brothers in the First World War and thought his son too young to enlist.

In the spring of 1941, I went to Fort St. James, intending to get a job in the mercury mine at Pinchi Lake. I could not get on steady at the mine for a month, but fortunately, landed a job with Orald Harrison, a fellow from Ootsa Lake. Orald was building boats at the Fort, and showed me the ins and outs of the job. (Later in life, this was a great help, as I built four boats of my own during my years as a guide and outfitter.)

After a month working with Orald, I went to work at the Pinchi Lake mercury mine. I had several jobs during my time there. First,

I worked on the bull gang, a crew that dug ditches and did any other work that involved a shovel. After this, I graduated to the smelter, where I wheeled out hot rock from which the mercury had been smelted. Wheeling slag (as it was called) was a hot job, and one I didn't care for. However, I soon had a chance to work in the mine, and was lucky to be teamed up with an old-timer named Slim Connor. He was great to work with, and taught me a lot; however, I realized later I still had a lot to learn.

After working for several months, I decided to buy a car. There was a First of July picnic and dance at Wistaria, and as I had a few days off, I decided to go. It was at this point that I received a difficult lesson in the School of Hard Knocks.

On the return trip from Wistaria, I rolled and totaled my car near Fraser Lake. This caused me to be late getting back to work, and I was fired on the spot.

At the time, I couldn't believe what was happening. A few days earlier, I'd been sitting on top of the world; suddenly, I didn't have a car or a job, and was flat broke. This was the only time in my life I was ever fired from a job, but I think it taught me a good lesson.

Luckily, I knew several people at Pinchi, and they gave me lodging until I was able to catch a ride to Vanderhoof. Again, I was lucky; an old farmer named Jock hired me to help put up hay. This farmer was a Scotsman and one of the nicest men I have ever met. He was a bachelor, but his house was spotless and he was an excellent cook.

We got along well. Jock was happy with my work and I was happy with the way he treated me. I stayed until we finished haying.

The old farmer then asked me to stay and work on the farm, but I had decided to join the army as soon as I was of age. It was difficult to leave Jock as he'd treated me so well, but on July 27, 1941 -- my eighteenth birthday -- I said goodbye to him and left for Prince George on the train.

I never saw the old Scotsman again, but I will always remember his kindness and the influence he had on my future. In the few months I had been away from home, I had received some hard knocks and some expensive lessons, but at the same time had made some good friends and found there are many kind people in this world.

CHAPTER THREE
The Years of Army Training

I was on the station platform in Vanderhoof waiting to board the train when a friend from home walked up to me. "Where are you going, son?" asked Paddy Carroll, whose daughters I had grown up with at Wistaria.

"I'm joining the army, Paddy," was my reply.

Paddy just shook his head. "Good luck, son, but remember Old Joe will screw them in the finals." He was referring, of course, to Joe Stalin, and I often thought of his remark during my five years in the army.

The day after seeing Paddy, I signed my life away for almost five years. Another young fellow who hailed from Alexandria (just south of Quesnel) joined at the same time, and the following day, he and I left Prince George by train for Vernon, where we received our basic training.

After arriving at my destination, I discovered I wasn't the only Northerner who'd recently enlisted. Indeed, there were several boys in camp from the region: Harry Moffatt (whom I'd met in Prince George), and Herb Dell from Quesnel. The three of us soon became friends, and chummed around with a couple of other boys, Reg Miller and Keith Robinson.

Even after the war, the five of us kept in touch -- until time or circumstances interfered. Harry, sadly enough, was killed in a traffic accident several years ago; I still visit his family. I'm also sorry to report that Reg Miller has passed on; I attended his memorial service in Merritt. We all lost contact with Keith over the last few years.

While our friendship came easily in Vernon, at least one aspect of basic training didn't. We were not accustomed to the blasts we got from our superiors. I had to control my temper. I really wanted to punch several of the officers and NCOs right on the ends of their noses. However, realizing this would not earn me any brownie points, I managed to keep my cool.

It was very hot in Vernon during August 1941. We were wearing shorts and spats. I remember standing, back to the sun, and feeling the skin peel off my legs. An obnoxious corporal stuck his nose about two inches from mine and snapped: "You dummy, can't you stand still?" I really had to talk to myself on this one, but again, managed to control my temper.

It's often said that "what goes around, comes around", and in my case, the old adage proved correct. Several years later, after serving in Italy and Southern France, I was sent to England as an instructor, and it was here that I had the pleasure of meeting this same contemptuous corporal. This time around, though, the circumstances were different; he was in my platoon, but I out-ranked him. I must say it was difficult to treat the man kindly.

This may seem odd, but as we all know, strange things often happen in times of war. In many cases, when a soldier was sent overseas during the Second World War, he lost his rank if it was not 'confirmed.' This was the reason my corporal friend was a lower rank than I when we met for a second time. My sergeants' stripes were bestowed under active duty and confirmed two months later, while the instructor from Vernon only earned confirmation on his corporal rating after arriving in England.

Yet all this, of course, was far in the future. While in Vernon, I tried to make the best of things. I was invited to visit the Ashfords who lived at Summerland. Mr. Ashford had formerly been the United Church minister in Burns Lake, and while there had once a month held services at the Wistaria Church.

As I had weekend leave, I arrived at the Ashfords' Summerland residence on a Friday evening. Well, who should answer the door but Mrs. Rist. She and daughter Jessie were staying there while the

The mountains of Tweedsmuir Park, as seen from our home on Ootsa Lake.

Friend and noted story-teller Paddy Carroll.

latter attended school.

I don't think Mrs. Rist trusted me at the time. In fact, I suspect she thought me a naughty boy -- when I was really just a young, red-blooded Canadian. Though she didn't allow me to take Jessie to the show, I still spent a pleasant weekend with them.

Some years later, my wife and I lived next door to Elmer and Monica Mohr. We saw Mrs. Rist often, as she was Monica's mother. One day, she was telling me that her granddaughter was only sixteen and crazy about boys. I couldn't help but comment.

"Mrs. Rist," I said, "the worst calling-down I ever got was for kissing *your* sixteen-year-old daughter."

She looked a little embarrassed. "Alan, as soon as I started to speak, I knew by the expression on your face that you had an answer for me." After that, we were great friends.

Mrs. Rist has since departed this world, but Jessie visits her cousin Alma Addison frequently. Elmer passed away at the age of ninety while visiting a daughter in Texas.

After the weekend in Summerland, it was back to basics -- basic training, that is. While in Vernon, though, we were given the opportunity to upgrade our education at trade school. I chose electricity, and found myself shipped off to Vancouver, where we were stationed in an old hotel. While learning the ins and outs of the electrical trade, we could take additional high school courses by correspondence if we wished, and I made the most of it.

After two semesters in Vancouver, we were shipped to Hamilton, Ontario for two more. When the course was completed, we received certificates as Class B electricians. This training really helped me in later years; in 1969, I obtained my Class B electrical contractors' licence, which I hold to this day.

While stationed at Hamilton I met and visited many of the Priest family's relatives, and enjoyed it immensely. Many years later, one of Charlie's cousins came with her husband and used my guiding services.

In Hamilton, a French-Canadian fellow had a barber shop across the street from the trade school. I remember he always had good stories to tell while cutting hair, and I went there whenever I needed a haircut -- sometimes just to hear him tell stories with his

Eastern accent. A few years ago, I was having my hair cut at Gene Vienneau's barber shop in Burns Lake, and during our conversation, I learned that the eloquent barber in Hamilton was Gene's father. It just goes to show you how small a world we live in!

As trade school ground to a close, my fellow troop mates and I began speculating on our next move. All speculation ended, however, when we were given two choices: Either go overseas with the Royal Canadian Service Corps, or join the First Special Service Force, a unique unit comprised of specially-trained Canadian and American soldiers. Several of us chose the latter, perhaps because we were informed that volunteers for the Force would not be subjected to kitchen duty. Little did we know what was in store for us.

No sooner had we said yes to the First Special Service Force than we were on a train headed for Helena, Montana, where the FSSF was mustering.

The training we received in Helena was tough, and I doubt anyone will ever forget it. Having been a participant, I can honestly say there were no dead-beats in The Force. Every move was double time, and punctuality was stressed regardless how tight the schedule. Some recruits could not meet the pace and were sent back to their original units.

The First Special Service Force officially came into being on June 20, 1942. Our commander was Col. Robert T. Frederick, a man respected by all Force members. You'd never find Col. Frederick behind a desk or at the rear during battle; indeed, he was wounded eight times and called a "stupid son-of-a-bitch" by some of his fellow officers. Yet he beat the odds, and was promoted to general at age thirty-seven.

Col. Frederick set the tone for all Force members during parachute training, when he made his first jump with only fifteen minutes of briefing. Seeing him do it made it difficult for the rest of us to refuse. Of course, there were some who couldn't or wouldn't jump, and they were immediately sent back to their original units.

I was very proud to be a member of The Force. In the slightly more than two years my troop mates and I spent together, we developed a comraderie envied by other units. Even though the FSSF consisted of Canadian and U.S. soldiers, its members shared a single identity and unity of purpose. There were very few problems in the ranks. We were simply "The Force."

After completing our initial training and receiving our parachute jump qualification badges, we were allowed to go into the town of Helena in the evenings and on weekends. In addition to its friendly residents, Helena was rich in beautiful girls; as a result, several members of The Force married Helena girls after the war. I still maintain contact with friends in that fair Montana town.

I t was with reluctance that we left Montana for Camp Bradford, where we received training in combat beach landings. The first few days in this new setting were spent learning how to climb over the sides of ships and into waiting landing craft -- all while wearing full gear. Proficiency was the objective; each time we went over the side, our 'loading' time improved. Eventually, a contingent from Third Regiment completed the exercise in a mere thirty-three seconds -- easily eclipsing the old record of fifty-two seconds, which had been set by the U.S. Marine Corps.

After receiving a rating of excellence throughout the training period, The Force proceeded to Fort Ethan Allen in Vermont. There, new recruits received instruction in parachute jumping while the rest of us got amphibious training on Lake Champlain.

By this time, there was a lot of talk about the Aleutians. Apparently, the Japanese had moved into the island chain, which put them too close to Alaska for comfort. The Kiska Force was training in California, preparing to invade the Aleutian Islands. General Marshall asked that the First Special Service Force be attached to the Kiska Force, and his request was granted.

By June 15, inspectors arrived at Fort Ethan Allen to evaluate The Force in terms of combat readiness. We weren't surprised to learn that in their opinion, The Force was more than capable of handling any physical hardship its members might encounter.

We headed west in short order, arriving at San Francisco's

Angel Island on July 3. Here, after being issued winter clothing, we were told The Force would be part of an amphibious force operating in northern waters. On July 9, The Force boarded two Liberty ships; two days later, it departed San Francisco for Adak Island.

For as long as I live, I shall never forget this trip to the back end of the world. The ocean was not kind to us land-lubbers; everyone was sick as the sea tossed, rolled, and pitched. We all thought the ship would break in half.

I was sick for five days. Yet despite the discomfort, hunger eventually drove me to the galley, where I thought I'd try a little breakfast. After taking one look at the greasy eggs they were dishing out -- and watching the soldier next to me vomit in his plate -- I decided to wait another day.

The sea eventually calmed, but many of us were weak for days.

Our commander, Col. Frederick, had flown to Adak and decided Amchitka Island would make a better camp, so on July 24, we landed there. Fog was ever-constant and the days lasted from four a.m. to ten p.m. It rained most of the time; the terrain was muddy, and we sunk to our ankles with every step. If I never see the Aleutians again, it will be too soon.

Eventually, the day of battle arrived. In preparation for the assault, Allied planes pounded Kiska with bombs; in one 24-hour period, 300,000 pounds of explosive were dropped on the island.

First and Third Regiments went ashore in landing craft and rubber boats. Under the original plan, Second Regiment was to parachute in after the initial landings. Luckily, though, we never had to jump. The Japanese, it was learned, had vacated the island under the cover of heavy fog. I guess the bombing was too much for them.

I think this was a lucky break for Second Regiment, as the navy's intelligence reports proved inaccurate. Our landing zone, we discovered later, consisted primarily of rough terrain interspersed with large rocks — and not flat sandy beach as the navy experts said. To make matters worse, these 'beaches' were covered to a depth of three or four feet with slippery kelp. Had we proceeded with the jump, casualties would have been high.

ABOVE & RIGHT: Training for the First Special Service Force in Helena, Montana.

First parachute jump. Good thing the fright doesn't show.

With no enemy opposing us, we were ordered to return to the United States. On the twenty-fourth of August, the First Special Service Force was homeward bound -- but only for a short while. The Allied command had plans for us in other parts of the world.

Upon arrival in San Francisco, we were given ten days leave. This didn't give me much time to get home, but I made it -- and was rewarded for my efforts with a case of measles. By the time I was well enough to return to The Force, the rest of my troop mates had moved on to Camp Patrick Henry in Virginia. I caught up with them there, and we received another bout of vigorous training. It kept us in shape for the next move.

On the twenty-eighth of October, we boarded the Empress of Scotland bound for Casablanca. This cruise was much better than the previous one, except for the food. We had two meals a day; most of the time, they consisted of mutton stew, and believe me, it isn't very appetizing when you find a round piece of gristle ringed with wool on your plate. I'm not exactly sure what part of the sheep's anatomy could produce such a disgusting tidbit, but one immediately springs to mind.

The food was bad enough, but to top it all off, at Casablanca we were loaded in box cars that had hauled sheep. By the time we got to Oran, we all smelled like the train's previous occupants. Since that time, I haven't even liked to hear the word 'sheep.'

Despite the accommodations, the train trip across Northern Africa was interesting. We passed many nomad settlements, and their inhabitants all turned out to see what was going on. It was unbelievable how these people lived.

We departed Oran, Algeria by ship on November 16, 1943, and arrived in Naples, Italy a mere three days later. Little did we realize the hell that lay in store for us.

Within weeks, hundreds of men would be dead or wounded. We were now in the war zone.

CHAPTER FOUR
Italy and Southern France

It was decided that Second Regiment of the First Special Service Force would assault Mount La Difensa in Italy. Patrols had been going out looking for the best assault route, and finally one was chosen. It would takc The Force over to the right of the hill, but required the scaling of a steep escarpment.

Though it presented our troops with several obstacles, this line of attack was chosen for its shock value; it was unlikely, our leaders speculated, that the Germans defending La Difensa would expect opposition from this direction.

We had been training hard for several days when the order came to assault the mountain. Everyone was ready, and on December 1, 1943, Second Regiment moved up with full gear to within a half-dozen miles of La Difensa's base. After getting off the trucks, we marched in darkness for six hours, slogging through mud and pouring rain to a spot that offered protection from German fire on the mountain top. While we dried clothing and checked weapons, Col. Frederick gave us a truly grim picture of what lay ahead.

First Regiment, we learned, was assigned as reserves. Third Regiment, meanwhile, was given double duty: its members were to serve either as litter-bearers for Second Regiment (a task that fell to First Battalion) or as reserves to be used when and where needed (Second Battalion). Second Regiment would lead the assault.

I was in Third Company, Second Regiment, and commanded by

Lt. Col. Tom McWilliam.

After what seemed like an eternity, The Force got the order to begin its final assault. We started the grueling climb of La Difensa itself, and quickly came to appreciate all the training we'd received in mountain climbing. The night was cold and rainy; we cursed and puffed our way up the hill, wondering when the fighting would begin. Dawn found us all in position, still concealed from the enemy. It stopped raining, and we were ordered to fix bayonets.

The sight before us was unreal; I can honestly say it was like walking into Hell. Allied artillery had started softening up the German positions at sunset the night before, and were still pounding away at the mountain top as we readied for our final assault. We learned later that 22,000 rounds were dropped on La Difensa during the night, and believe me, it showed.

We were told to hold our fire until six a.m., but some men slipped while moving into position and sent gravel rolling down on the Germans. Flares went up, and all hell broke loose. The battle for La Difensa was on.

The fighting was ferocious. Both officers and enlisted men were involved in hand-to-hand combat atop La Difensa -- a real rarity in the Second World War. Fortunately, as a machine-gunner, I wasn't involved in the close-quarters stuff; however, I was pinned down by German machine guns for nearly an hour, and only able to move my position after some of our troops dislodged the enemy.

Because two previous assaults on La Difensa by other units had failed, Fifth Army staff anticipated it would take three or four days to secure the mountain. We did it in less than four hours. Our success, I think, can be attributed to the element of surprise and superior fire-power; our sudden appearance on the mountain caught the Germans flat-footed, while our Tommy guns and submachine guns produced a hail of bullets.

Though we succeeded in accomplishing what others had failed to do, the victory on La Difensa was bitter-sweet and achieved only with much sadness and loss of friends. Heavy mortar and artillery fire took its toll; Lt. Col. McWilliam was killed, and

Major Ed Thomas was wounded with a bayonet. Dozens of others lay dead or wounded.

The battle etched images in my memory that can never be erased. One in particular stands out, and it can only be described as both horrible and unfortunate.

In an effort to gain an insight into future enemy troop movements, we were told to take as many prisoners as possible during the assault. With this in mind, when a group of our men took a machine gun nest near my position, they called for the enemy's surrender. A group of German soldiers emerged waving white flags, yet when one of our officers went to take the men prisoner, he was shot and killed.

The results were as predictable as they were bloody. The German soldiers, even those who'd taken no part in the treachery, were instantly mowed down by machine gun fire from our troops. Needless to say, the incident ended our campaign to take prisoners.

I can't forget how, in this instance, one thoughtless action by a German officer resulted in the loss of many German lives and that of at least one good FSSF officer. It wasn't the last time this would happen, either; during my five years in the army, I witnessed several incidents in which one self-centred individual sacrificed the lives of many good men simply for the sake of prestige or self-esteem.

When I think about the stupidity of war and the actions of some so-called human beings who participate in it, I can only hope and pray we aren't involved in another global conflict. These days, though, a few more leaders like Hitler are emerging to threaten world peace. How frightening.

Though we'd taken La Difensa, there were adjoining mountains from which the Germans could observe our movements. And so the fighting continued.

After six days of bloody battle, the Difensa-Camino-Maggiore group was in Allied hands. The Force had lost one-third of its men in casualties; in total, there were more than seventy dead, three hundred wounded, and nine missing in action. More than one

A group of First Special Service Force members on a few days of rest in Italy. That's me on the far left, my good friend Ray Elizonda on the far right.

Yours Truly atop Mount
La Difensa in Italy.

It was on this hill that I injured my knee during a battle in 1944. The ridge in the background forms the border between Italy and France. (Reg Blackwell Photo - May 1995)

Here I'm showing my sons Reg and Neil where I sustained the injury in 1944. (Reg Blackwell Photo)

hundred of our soldiers had succumbed to exhaustion. Col. Frederick was wounded twice, but carried on.

During heavy fighting, I'd helped lay one of my buddies on a stretcher. He'd been hit in the throat by shrapnel and I never thought he'd survive. For more than forty years, I thought he'd died in Italy; you can imagine my surprise and happiness when, at a force get-together not long ago, I was reunited with him once more. The wound impaired my friend's speech, but I'm pleased to say he is still very much alive.

The 142nd Infantry finally relieved us and we came down the God-forsaken mountain never wanting to look back. We'd all seen enough blood, both ours and the enemy's.

We now had time to rest and consider the events of the past few days. It seemed no matter how hard I tried, I couldn't forget the boys who'd been killed or wounded -- nor the scene atop La Difensa after our first battle. Dead Germans had lain everywhere, and among them, the bodies of our own fallen comrades. Punctuating this grisly sight was the menacing flicker of Allied artillery from the valley below; not to be outdone, the Germans responded with 'Screaming Meemies', those six-barreled rocket launchers that, while none too effective, made a hell of a noise and demoralized almost everyone. At some point that day, I found myself comparing the carnage around me to the view from my parents' property in Wistaria -- and praying that some day I'd again experience the peace and quiet of home.

The Force received several assignments in the mountains that winter, and our casualties were high. It was cold, and the land was blanketed with heavy snow. Many of our men suffered from frost bite, while others contracted trench foot (a nasty ailment that landed me in hospital for five days).

Finally, we were relieved -- and none too soon. The Force spent ten days in Santa Maria, and passes were granted to Naples. During this time, our unit was also honoured for its victories in battle. Key promotions were handed out; Col. Frederick became a Brigadier General, and a few sergeants received commissions in the field. A fair number of enlisted men also rose in rank, including 'yours truly', who suddenly found himself promoted to sergeant.

Shortly thereafter, we headed for Anzio. Closer to Rome and behind German lines, this new landing site pitted us against four German divisions commanded by Field Marshal Albert Kesselring.

The Force moved into position along the Mussolini Canal. Ordered to hold the ground at all costs, we dug in and covered our shelters with logs, tin, and anything else we could find. In the end, our preparations undoubtedly saved many lives, because it wasn't long before the Germans started dropping 'basket bombs' on us. When these container-like parcels hit the ground, they'd break open and scatter phosphorus bombs the size of eggs everywhere -- severely burning anything with which they came in contact.

Of course, we didn't just sit in our holes and take whatever the enemy hurled at us. Every night, we'd blacken our faces with camouflage paint and send patrols into the German lines. On these sorties, we'd harass the Germans unmercifully, then leave our own unique 'calling cards' -- stickers that bore the spearhead insignia of The Force and the German phrase *Da Dicke Ende Kommt Noch* ("The worst is yet to come") -- on his positions and dead. Our 'calling cards' and blackened faces apparently wreaked psychological havoc among the German troops, because they began referring to us simply as "The Black Devils." At the very least, we got them thinking, as the diary of one German attests. "These Black Devils are all around us," the Wehrmacht soldier wrote prior to capture. "We don't know where they will strike next."

It was on one of these night patrols that I had perhaps my worst scare of the war. It involved a German mine nicknamed 'Bouncing Betty' by Allied troops because when triggered, it jumped about four feet in the air before exploding and throwing shrapnel everywhere.

My patrol was working its way out through a mine field at night when I stepped on a 'Betty.' Feeling that horrifying click as its trigger depressed, I thought: "This is it." Much to my relief, though, the mine turned out to be a dud. Troop mate Ray Elizonda was behind me at the time, and we couldn't believe our luck. (Years later, at a Force reunion, Ray turned to my wife Marion and said: "Did this guy ever tell you how lucky he can be?" Of course, she didn't know what he was talking about, because I never shared any war experiences with my family.)

Our tour at Anzio was grueling. The Force was defending a large area with about two thousand men; though vastly outnumbered and subjected to horrific artillery barrages from the enemy, we held our ground. In later years, our somewhat unorthodox tactics and nearly unmatched military record inspired the popular book and movie *The Devil's Brigade*. At Anzio, though, our nightly raids served a more useful purpose; indeed, it has been suggested that they led the enemy to over-estimate our numbers, and probably discouraged him from mounting a deliberate attack.

Thinking over battles fought and comrades we lost, I often wonder how some of us survived almost unscathed.

I lost two buddies at Anzio; we'd trained together from Day One. Bert was one of them. One night, he came to me and said: "Blackie, I'm picked for patrol tonight. I can't refuse, but I have a bad feeling that I won't be coming back." His words proved prophetic; when the patrol returned, he wasn't with it. I never learned what happened to him, and he is still listed as "missing in action."

A few days after Bert disappeared, our platoon was moving up a nearly barren valley when we came under mortar fire. My other buddy, Art Knapp, was only a few feet from me. When the shells started falling, we all dived for cover, which unfortunately was scarce. Screams and yells filled the air, competing with the sounds of exploding shells. Many men were wounded and several were killed, including Art. Though at least one mortar shell had landed squarely between Art and I, he was the one to die. I didn't receive so much as a scratch.

The Force was relieved at Anzio in early May 1944. We were given a few days to lick our wounds, then prepare for the breakout and capture of Rome.

At 6:30 a.m. on May 24, 1944, we were headed for Italy's capital. It was a tough fight all the way, but on June 4 at approximately six in the morning, the First Special Service Force entered the fabled city. Though I didn't know it at the time, Cyril Shelford was with Canadians entering it from the other side.

Its goal achieved, The Force now received a much-deserved rest at Lake Albano. We also received the bad news that General Frederick had been given a new command, the 1ST Airborne Task Force. Col. Walker of Third Regiment took over command of the First Special Service Force.

When our R & R ended, we headed back to Anzio and boarded ships for Santa Maria Castablate. After getting reinforcements and some vigorous training, The Force was assigned to the Seventh Army, which at the time was preparing for yet another invasion.

The jumping off point was to be Corsica. However, problems with my feet and legs landed me in hospital there, and I didn't rejoin my comrades until late August. By that time, they were already operating in Southern France.

We fought our way along the Riviera from Cannes to Menton, in the process taking hundreds of prisoners -- many of them young. We did encounter grim resistance in some areas, though, particularly in the mountains north of Menton. It was during this time that I earned another trip to hospital.

My misfortune occurred when Second Regiment had taken Castelar and Third Company was working its way towards the Italian border. The terrain in which we operated was steep and included many small cliffs, and it made progress difficult. During the climb, we came under heavy fire from German machine guns and dove for cover. In the ensuing scramble, our platoon officer was wounded and two of us fell over a small cliff. We were both hurt badly enough to require hospitalization.

Though I was only in hospital a short time, the injury precluded me from more active duty. I spent the rest of my time with The Force as a radio and telephone operator. My knee was in bad shape then, and has given me trouble since. In later years, I received a small disability pension in recognition of the injury.

Once, during my time as a radio and telephone operator, I was given a room full of prisoners to guard. They were only children; some looked less than sixteen years old. Yet despite their situation -- or perhaps because of it -- they appeared content to sit and eat

C-rations while awaiting transportation to another facility. (In retrospect, I think the C-rations were the first real food these kids had seen in days.)

When assigned to guard these poor kids, I'd already been on duty for many hours. As a result, despite my best efforts, I dozed off sometime during the night. I awoke with a start, but much to my relief found the German prisoners chatting happily among themselves and paying little attention to me. With only a Tommy gun to hold off the thirty of them, I could have been in real trouble; I guess, though, they'd all had their fill of fighting.

November 1944 was a time of change for The Force. The strategists decided they no longer needed small assault units such as ours; as a result, we were told the FSSF would be disbanded, and its members either assigned to new units or given jobs as instructors. It was difficult to believe that despite its glorious history, our unit was being dispersed. During its existence, The Force had sustained nearly 3,000 casualties; 2,300 had been wounded, and another 400 were listed either as dead or missing in action.

On the fifth of December 1944, the last parade of the First Special Service Force was held at Villeneuve-Loubet, France. It was a sad day; strong men wept as they bid farewell to their comrades. I was with a group of NCOs going to England as instructors, and it wasn't easy saying goodbye to men I'd fought beside for years.

The events of December 5, 1944 represented the final chapter in The Force's illustrious history, and spelled the end of active fighting for me. I thanked God I'd survived nineteen months of hell. As I lay in bed that night, I thought of the many friends I'd made and the many who were gone. Yet I also contemplated the peace, quiet, and beauty of Ootsa Lake and the mountains beyond, praying once more that someday soon I'd be able to return.

I couldn't help but wonder what my future assignment had in store for me. Being an instructor sounded scary, but by this time I'd had my fill of fighting. "From now on," I thought, laying in the darkness, "I will be a lover, not a fighter." I was looking forward to England and meeting for the first time many of my relatives.

A post card I picked up in Rome. The Coliseum is an impressive sight.

It's true that as members of the First Special Service Force, we suffered through some tough fighting and the loss of many friends -- as did most everyone who served on the front lines during World War Two. Yet not all our wartime experiences were bad ones; indeed, we saw some great sights and met many interesting people.

Rome, which I visited as a member of The Force, has a lot to offer anyone interested in history. The Vatican, for example, is an unbelievable place, and the same can be said of the old Coliseum, which is located in another part of the city. I saw the Coliseum in 1944, and remember it well. At the time, as I looked down into what were once the pits and lion pens of this infamous structure, imagining the horror and cruelty inflicted on humans there more than two millennia earlier was all too easy.

CHAPTER FIVE
England

I arrived in England in early December 1944, after what proved to be a rather nerve-wracking voyage. Our ship was attacked by a submarine in the Bay of Biscay, but luckily, the destroyers escorting us sank the enemy submersible before we were torpedoed.

After disembarking in Prestwick, Scotland, we boarded a train and traveled to Aldershot. Here, we were assigned to different training camps. I was being sent to Petworth in Southern England, but not before a ten-day leave. We all had to undergo medical examinations before taking our R & R, but after a few days, I was on my way to Cambridge to see my relatives.

I traveled by train, and it was late at night when I arrived at my destination. I had my Uncle Herbert and Aunt Irene's address and had phoned them to say I was coming, but it was nevertheless one a.m. when I finally knocked on their door.

Aunt Irene answered. "You must be Alan," she said, looking at me. "Last week, Fred knocked me up at one a.m. and now you knock me up at the same hour." I thought her use of the phrase 'knocked up' more than a little funny at the time, but later learned it's simply an expression used by the English to describe being awakened during the night.

The next day, I was given the addresses of all my relatives on Mother's side, and began visiting them. First, I stayed two days with my grandparents, the Spicers. They treated me royally, and I enjoyed myself so much that I stayed with them on many subsequent weekend leaves.

My grandparents told me how to find other kin. My Aunt Florence (Floss) lived only a short distance away, so I visited her next. My uncle was an officer in the Royal Air Force at the time, so I didn't get to see him. Still, I had the opportunity to become very close friends with my Aunt Floss and my cousins Eileen and Muriel. From here on, I had a grand time whenever I was on leave.

One Saturday night, I escorted seven girls, six of whom were my cousins, to a dance in Cambridge. "Canada," the fellow taking admission at the door asked, "are all these girls with you?"

I replied that they were, to which he responded: "Well, if you can get along with seven bloody women, you can go in free."

I also stayed two days with my Uncle Jack Spicer. He and wife Dorie only had one daughter, Valerie, and we have all remained close over the years.

At the time, Valerie was working at a paper mill in Sawston. I was to meet her after work, but as I stood outside the factory, a pompous Englishman made some nasty remarks about my waiting for girls. He was sitting on a bicycle at the time, but not for long; I let him have it, a good hard right to the jaw. He and his bicycle went flying, and no one else had anything to say after that. Later, I learned this rude ass was Valerie's boss.

In the ten days I was on leave, I had a wonderful time. I met most of Mother's relatives and a few of Dad's. It was with reluctance, therefore, that I returned to Aldershot and accepted assignment to Petworth training camp.

I arrived in my new digs about four p.m., was promptly given quarters and told I'd meet my superior (a Capt. Norton) later. I was lying on my bunk when a message came for me to report to the camp theatre.

Upon entering, I was met by Capt. Norton, who asked me to give a talk on the fighting in Italy. I was stunned; there were more than two hundred men present, and I had nothing prepared. I gave a talk of sorts, but how I got through it, I'll never know.

I had a chat with the captain afterwards, told him I thought he'd been unfair. He was very cooperative and agreed to send me to

RIGHT: Grandad and Grandmother Spicer as I remember them in 1945.

BELOW: My grandparents' house in Duxford, England.

LEFT: Some of my relatives. They kept me on the straight and narrow during my time in England. (Pictured are: Valerie Spicer, E. Curtis, Phyllis Norfield, Uncle Roland Spicer, Rita Norfield, Marie Spicer, and Aunt Jean.)

Chuck Van Tine (right) and I in London, 1945.

public speaking school for a week. This was a great experience.

The class included soldiers of all rank, and no distinctions were made between officers and enlisted men. I soon learned that many of the officers had more difficulty with public speaking than I, and this gave me more confidence.

At this point, I was given a platoon of men to train, and I had the pleasure of being reunited with the obnoxious corporal from Vernon.

I enjoyed my time as an instructor, particularly its short work days, good food, and weekend leaves. I went to Cambridge almost every weekend, and -- in addition to visiting my grandparents -- spent a lot of my time (including Christmas 1944) with my cousins. There were a dozen of them, all girls. As you can imagine, it wasn't difficult to find a girlfriend during my time in England, as my cousins introduced me to new girls each weekend.

It was in Duxford, where my grandparents lived, that I chanced upon a pub called The Plow. The owner, it turned out, was an old friend of my father. It was a fortuitous meeting; for use during subsequent visits to Duxford, the publican gave me a card that read: "Free beer for this soldier."

Over the winter months, we trained troops for combat, providing special instruction in the use of weapons employed by The Force. Despite the fact that we heard almost daily rumours of weakening resistance in Europe, the Germans continued to inflict heavy casualties on Allied forces there. Not much, it seemed, had changed in the Pacific, either; the Japanese were still raising hell on a score of islands. We all wondered how much longer the bloody war would last. I still prayed, as I'm sure many soldiers did, that it would end and we'd all return home.

Perhaps our collective prayers were heard, because by the end of April it was obvious the war in Europe would soon be over. As one might imagine, it was with great enthusiasm that we celebrated victory on May 8, 1945. I was in London on VE Day, and doubt I'll ever see another celebration like it. In a matter of hours, I met up with Chuck Van Tine, Dick Schrieber, Chummy McPhail and Clarence Saunders -- all boys from the Burns Lake area. Dick, Chuck, and I then looked up Marion Keefe, who was with the air force in London. It was great to see these friends from home.

To celebrate victory, all Canadian forces overseas received two weeks' leave. Though they had to be taken in rotation, everyone got holidays; I used mine to visit relatives yet again.

Toward the end of my leave to Cambridge, Cyril Shelford called and said he was coming to visit. He arrived as planned, and it wasn't long before we were sitting in The Red Lion pub having a few drinks. With 'holidays' almost over, we decided to call my commanding officer and get them extended.

Needing a valid reason for requesting additional leave, Cyril and I came up with the half-baked story that he was getting married and wanted me as best man. Two air force officers were sitting with us, and -- believing Cyril was about to get hitched -- had been buying one round of drinks after another. By this time, none of us was feeling any pain; yet despite our inebriated state, we proceeded to make the customary phone call.

Because we were trying to reach an army camp, our call had to go through military headquarters. I vaguely remember having difficulty making the connections, and the folks on the other end of the phone asking a lot of questions.

Somehow, we stumbled through the process. When a British officer in London asked why we hadn't made the necessary arrangements sooner, Cyril calmly answered: "How could I? I only met the girl today."

"Are you an R.A.F. man?" the officer enquired.

"No," replied Cyril proudly. "I'm a Canadian."

"Oh," said the British officer, as if Cyril's answer was to be expected. With that, though, he immediately put us through to my commanding officer, who (much to my surprise) extended my leave without a moment's hesitation.

But the adventure didn't end there. The next day, Cyril and I were back in the same pub with my uncle and cousin. Who should show up but the two Royal Air Force officers who'd been so friendly the night before? This time, they'd didn't offer us anything more than a dirty look. We didn't mind, though, because we certainly enjoyed our leave together.

Around the same time, I was making the trip to Cambridge and by chance met yet another relative. I was sitting on the bus minding my own business when a pretty young girl sat down beside me. "You must be my cousin Alan," she said, wasting no time. "I know you're a paratrooper and a sergeant, so when I saw your boots, stripes, and wings, I knew it had to be you."

I told her all angels had wings, but she told me I didn't look like an angel.

This sharp-witted girl proved to be Babs Evans, a daughter of my mother's youngest sister. After our chance meeting on the bus, I went home with her and met the rest of the family: Taff, Betty, Pam, Tony, and baby David. I even had the honour of being David's godfather when he was christened. Tony and David are the only ones left living; Tony and family live in Surrey, and David and family live in New Westminster. Sadly, Babs died of cancer a year after I came home from the war; her parents passed away only a few years later. Pam married a U.S. soldier and moved to Tacoma, where she developed multiple sclerosis and passed away last year.

Upon my return from leave, it was obvious that our training sessions would take a different focus. With the war in Europe over, the troops under our instruction were prepared for police duties in Occupied Germany. To emphasize this shift in priorities, I was given a platoon of new men. It was planned that on August 10, 1945 -- when our training was complete -- we'd go to Germany.

I continued training men for occupation until the first part of August. I had one final weekend leave to Cambridge on my twenty-second birthday, and spent it with my relatives. Though I didn't know it, this was the last time we'd see each other for many years -- and the last time I would see my grandparents.

After arriving back in camp, I was told we'd be leaving for Germany shortly. Yet during the first week of August, just as we were getting ready to ship out, a message came for me to report to the office. Thinking that something bad had happened, I ran all the way there; yet what I heard I could scarcely believe.

"Sergeant, you are a very lucky man," the corporal at the desk informed me. "There's a Liberator bomber flying from Prestwick,

Scotland to Montreal. It will take a group of men picked at random, and your name has been drawn. Get your things together. You leave tomorrow for Scotland."

I was overwhelmed with emotion, and cried as I went back to the barracks. Everyone thought I had received bad news from home.

Next morning, I said goodbye to Capt. Norton. He was a great boss, and I had a lot of respect for him. I then went to see my platoon, men I'd been training for a month. That's when leaving England became difficult.

The men begged me to give up my seat on the Liberator and go to Germany with them. I gathered this was their first day with a new sergeant, and the fool was making them press their shoe laces. Having encountered this type of stupidity earlier in my army career, I felt sorry for the men, but had absolutely no intention of throwing away my chance to go home.

Two days later I was on the plane heading for Montreal. I held an inside seat, while the aisle spot was taken by a major, a doctor from Winnipeg who was also homeward bound. It was a beautiful flight until we neared Newfoundland, at which time one of the plane's motors started acting up.

I wasn't overly concerned, as there were four motors on the Liberator; besides, having served in the paratroops, I was accustomed to flying. However, when the disabled motor finally quit altogether, a fellow across the aisle went berserk. "We're going to crash," he screamed. "We'll all be killed. What are we going to do?"

Much to my surprise, the major next to me jumped up, smacked the silly fellow, and told him to shut up. "Act like a soldier instead of a baby," he added forcefully.

The major's actions calmed everyone, and we flew on to Montreal with three motors and no further incidents. The fellow who'd gone berserk was an officer, and I suspect he was suffering from shell shock. Regardless of rank or disability, though, I was happy to see the major smarten him up.

After fourteen hours on a Liberator, it was a very tired group of boys that arrived in Montreal. I was happy to put my feet on

Canadian soil.

Though relieved to at last be homeward bound, to this day I have many fond memories of England -- and most of them involve my relatives. I only met a few of Dad's kin at the time, but remember two cousins on his side of the family taking me to see their mother.

The woman was sick in bed on the day in question, yet managed to sit up and make proper conversation the entire time I was there. Apparently, there was a reason for her remaining upright; unbeknownst to us at the time, she'd just settled herself on a bed pan when I was ushered into the room. The grand dame was quite upset by this incursion, but I never knew it until my cousin Betty told me on the phone a few years ago.

I have not seen Betty since, though I trust not because of our social miscue so many years ago.

CHAPTER SIX
Back in Canada

After a good night's rest in Montreal, I boarded a train for Vancouver. The major who slapped the soldier during the flight from England was also on board, bound for Winnipeg. Along the way I befriended an army girl headed for Vancouver. A corporal in the CWACs, she was a very nice person and proved welcome company on the trip across Canada.

There was another army girl on board with a friend, so we played cards and other games. We also sang a lot of songs, and had a truly enjoyable time. It's difficult to explain how happy I was to be back in Canada, particularly after having thought so many times that I might never see home again.

The trip across the prairies was very dusty. The train was old, and fine grit seeped in everywhere. We were dirty, and as army personnel, we only had two changes of clothing -- which didn't give us much opportunity to present a professional appearance. Despite the conditions, we tried to look decent.

We were allowed off the train briefly in Calgary, and I couldn't believe what happened next. While walking down the street, a female military police sergeant stopped us and charged the girls with a clothing violation because their outfits weren't clean and pressed. The incident probably represents the one and only time I've been impolite to a woman. She didn't have much to say when I was finished. The fellow with me was a corporal, and he never

The mountains and lake I was so pleased to see upon my return to Ootsa Lake in 1945. I can now look at them every day from my patio.

said a word at the time. Later, however, he commented: "I'm sure glad that you are of equal rank to that bitch."

The incident reminded me of a story I heard while in England. There, the interior of each train car is divided into compartments that seat four people on two benches facing each other. An aisle runs down one side of the car, with the compartments on the other; every compartment has a door and window opening into the aisle, and another window through which passengers can view the passing scenery.

On one occasion, an American soldier entered the train and found all compartments full except one, which contained two men, a snobbish English lady, and a small dog. It was apparent the dog belonged to the lady, as it lounged contentedly on the seat beside her.

With no place to sit, the G.I. entered and politely asked the woman if she would move her dog. "No," replied the lady, her aristocratic nose in the air. "My dog has the seat, and you can stand, Yankee."

Provoked by the rude remark, the American grabbed the dog and unceremoniously dumped it out the window and into the aisle. Yet as he settled into the now-vacant seat, he noticed one of the compartment's other occupants was a British colonel.

"I'm sorry, sir," he apologized hastily to the high-ranking Brit. "Did I do the right thing?"

"No," replied the Colonel sternly, "wrong bitch, wrong window."

Flabbergasted, the dog-owner jumped up and went to retrieve her pet. It was only then that the colonel smiled.

Oh, if only things had gone so well with the MP in Calgary. Yet despite the woman's nit-picking, we continued on our journey and finally arrived in Vancouver. It was here that the four of us parted company, and I've not seen nor heard of the others since. Thinking it over, I can't believe we never took the time to exchange addresses; I suppose, though, that we were so glad to be going home that none of us ever thought about it.

I reported to Army Military Depot #11, spent a couple of days resting, and then headed off for thirty days' leave. I arrived in Burns Lake to hear that the war with Japan had ended. It was VJ Day, August 15, 1945.

My brother Stanley and sister Millie met me at the station, and it was an emotional reunion. Stan had been twelve years old when I left home, but was now an adult. I had not seen Millie since my last leave home. I'm not ashamed to say that we all shed a few tears as we got in the car and headed for Wistaria.

When we crested the hill at Ootsa Lake, I glimpsed the shining water and rugged mountains that so many times in the past three years I'd thought I might never see again. Overcome with emotion, I had a difficult time holding back tears. The view was a beautiful one, and I thanked God for allowing me to survive five years of war -- nineteen months of it on the front line. I felt very lucky.

Mother had a great meal awaiting us at Wistaria. Many times while away, I'd dreamed of Mom's home-cooked meals, and at last I was able to enjoy one. It was wonderful to be home again.

I spent several days giving Mother and Dad news of England. Neither of them had been back to their homeland since coming to Canada.

Mother was pleased that I had spent a lot of time with her parents. Unfortunately, I didn't have the opportunity to spend time with Dad's, as they'd passed away even before I went overseas.

A week or so after arriving home, I looked up old friends. Because I was one of the first to return from the war, people were anxious to talk to me, particularly the parents of boys still away.

It was with sadness that I learned several local boys had been killed, while others had been wounded. Hugh Shelford, for example, had lost an arm while overseas and even spent time as a prisoner of war. As I visited the parents of friends who'd become casualties of the conflict, I again counted my blessings. I was fortunate to have survived.

During the month I spent at home, I visited everyone possible and enjoyed several parties. One of these parties was at Orald and Maude Harrison's. I remember dancing with Cecille Carroll on a gravel beach; it was a poor dance floor, but we had a lot of fun and it was a great change from army life.

Eventually, however, the time came for me to return to Vancouver, where I would have to await my discharge from the army. On the day I left, Scotty McIvor -- who'd lived at Arthur Shelford's for several years prior to the war -- came home to Wistaria. He'd married a Scottish girl while overseas, and planned to settle at Streatham.

Sadly enough, his dreams were never realized. The first news I received upon arrival in Vancouver was that Scotty -- who'd survived five years of active duty -- had been killed in a hunting accident at Ootsa Lake.

Back in army camp, I was again given sergeant's duties and spent six weeks at the old grind. However, I wasted little time making new friends, one of whom was Capt. Jack Reed. I spent some enjoyable times with the Reed family in Vancouver; later, Jack became a school teacher at Francois Lake, and his son Keith still owns a business in Burns.

I also met a girl from Francois Lake who happened to be

working in Vancouver at the time. We both loved dancing, and spent several evenings together in this manner. She also made me acquainted with other people who became friends.

On October 11, I finally received my discharge from active duty. A few of my superiors tried convincing me to stay in the army, but by this time I'd tolerated all the army life I could stand. With discharge in hand, I was free to do as I pleased.

Shortly after leaving the army, I was offered an electrician's job with Shell Oil in Chile. I might have accepted the offer if the company had given me more time at home, but they were adamant that I leave immediately. Of course, after so many years overseas, I wasn't prepared to leave quite so quickly; I came back to Ootsa Lake instead, and with the exception of short periods, have been here ever since.

We had an enjoyable Christmas 1945 in Wistaria. This was my first Christmas at home in five years, and it was a great day for me. Indeed, with the war over, the future seemed bright.

During the winter of '46, other soldiers came home, and a celebration was held each time one returned. I must say that we consumed far too much alcohol that winter. Liquor was rationed; gin was the easiest to get, so we drank gin and apple juice, or lemon gin and apple juice. We drank gallons of this junk that winter.

I really played the field with girls in the winter of '46, and so did the other boys. Yet I did give some thought to what my granddad Spicer said to me while watching Cyril and I strut our stuff overseas. "You Canadians are daft," he said at the time. "I only had one woman in my life, and that's the one I married."

Although we did devote much of our energies to girl-chasing, we managed to work a little in our spare time. Myles, Cyril, and I worked in a mill all winter. In April 1946, I went to work for the B.C. Forest Service in Burns Lake. I started as a dispatcher in the office, but was soon patrolman and later assistant ranger.

I worked for the forest service until September 1, 1946, when the grass looked greener on the other side of the hill. As an assistant ranger, I was getting $155 a month at a time when sawmill workers were making $10 a day, so I quit and went

RIGHT: Marion's brother and parents.

BELOW: Marion (foreground) and her sisters in later years.

The wedding of Alan Blackwell and Marion Anderson, Sept. 6, 1946. That's brother Stan Blackwell on the far left (he was my best man) and Marion's sister Helen Anderson (bridesmaid) on the far right.

Marion and I with children Reg (foreground) and Nadine at our farm on Ootsa Lake.

logging.

Two months later, the salary for an assistant ranger increased to $250 a month. Dad was furious with me for quitting.

Several 'factors' played a part in my decision to change careers, and as you might guess, one of them was female. Yet this wasn't just any ordinary 'female'; after going out with many of them during the winter, I started dating Marion Anderson, a girl who worked at a bakery in Burns Lake.

At the time, Marion was staying with her grandmother at Danskin. Having just bought a car, it seemed natural that I drive the young lady home on a regular basis -- which I did. Well, I guess I was hooked, because Marion and I set our wedding date for September 6, 1946.

Of course, with wedding bells set to chime, I felt the need to make more money -- hence the switch from forestry to logging, which seemed a good idea at the time. I jokingly maintain I've been under 'rule of thumb' since my engagement to Marion, but admittedly, it's been anything but unpleasant.

Dad did not like many of the girls I went out with, but he liked Marion immediately. She was easily embarrassed, and Dad loved it. It so happened that Dad had just returned home from the hospital when I took Marion home to visit, and he couldn't wait to tell her a story he heard while there.

The way Dad told the story, it seems a certain Mr. Brown's wife was in hospital expecting a baby. As Mr. Brown worked in a factory with a lot of girls and knew he'd be teased, the expectant father arranged for word of his child's birth to be delivered by code. When the baby had been born, the hospital was to call the factory and say: "Your wife has baked a cake for you."

Finally, Mr. Brown received his encrypted message, though not necessarily the one he expected. "Mr. Brown," stated the hospital worker, "your wife has baked two cakes for you: one is plain, and the other is garnished with nuts."

Poor Marion; she never knew what was coming. To this day, I can see the expression on her face when the punch line finally hit home. Dad, meanwhile, laughed like crazy -- as he always did at his own jokes.

Despite this inauspicious introduction to my family, Marion didn't call off the wedding. We were married at the United Church in Burns Lake, with a reception at Francois Lake and a dance at Grassy Plains hall.

The dance proved unforgettable. My newly-acquired brother-in-law had too many drinks, took my car and knocked hay shocks over in Bill Bickle's hay field. In the process, he must have punched a hole through the fuel tank, because when we were ready to go home, the vehicle was out of gas.

Because Marion's dad only had a small car, there wasn't room in it for all of us and our presents. Being a young couple without many worldly possessions, Marion and I didn't want to leave the gifts behind, so we decided to stay. Our wedding night was spent on a bench in the Grassy Plains hall, with Marion's parents sleeping on another bench nearby. After daylight, Marion's father towed us home, which at the time was a fully-furnished cabin I'd built on property owned by Wilton Barker.

Marion and I have received plenty of ribbing over this incident, but if the truth be known, I could have killed my brother-in-law at the time. I'm sure there are more pleasant things to do on one's wedding night than sleep on a hard wooden bench with your in-laws close by.

For the Blackwells, 1946 proved a busy year in the wedding department. My sister Millie was married in October of '46 to Bill Durban, and they raised a family of three girls and a boy (Pat, Arlene, Rhonda, and Brian). All Bill and Millie's children are married and have families of their own now, though they continue to live in the Lakes District. Millie is still doing relatively well, but I'm sorry to say that Bill is not.

But I digress. Prior to my wedding, I'd bought a sawmill in partnership with Wilton, and I worked with him for several months. Eventually, though, a conflict of personalities made it impossible for Wilton and I to remain partners. I sold out to him and went to work for my father-in-law, who had a sawmill at Eight Mile on the Babine Road.

My job at the Eight Mile mill involved falling trees with Mac Anderson using a six-foot crosscut saw. If I slowed down, Mac would tell me about the Frenchman he'd worked with whose favourite saying was: "I don't mind you dragging your feet, but please don't ride the saw."

I enjoyed the job and worked there for the remainder of 1947. In the spring, I went into partnership on another sawmill, this time with my brother-in-law Bill Bennett (who'd married Florence, Marion's older sister).

We moved to Ootsa Lake and sawed lumber on Bill's property during that summer and fall. Marion and I rented a cabin from McNeils and were living there when our first son, Reginald Keith

Blackwell, was born on August 23, 1947. (Marion, by this time, had gone to town and stayed with her mother.)

Reg's birth was cause for celebration, as he was the first grandson to be born on either side of the family. Upon hearing the news, Marion's Dad and I went to the Legion in Burns Lake and proceeded to disgust our respective wives by getting drunk and then sick.

In wake of this incident, there were at least two very quiet households in the Lakes District for a week or so. The Anderson house was exceptionally quiet after Agnes learned that during the celebration, husband Mac had provided the Legion's mixed audience with a spirited rendition of the off-colour army poem *Mrs. Murphy's Farting Party*. Though we thought it a charming little ditty at the time, it definitely wasn't suitable for recitation in front of women.

Such behavior was unusual for Mac, who seldom told an off-colour joke and swore with even greater rarity. It must have been the booze!

After Marion and Reg came home, we moved to a larger house at Ootsa Lake and I worked in the mill on Bill's property until fall. We then acquired some timber; Bill hauled logs with a team of horses and sleigh, while I ran the sawmill. We had an exceptionally good winter and made what was 'big money' in those days.

During the winter of 1948, Jock McIvor's widow came out from Scotland to dispose of her property at Streatham. I met with her, negotiated a price, and then bought the property with assistance from the Veterans Land Act. Marion and I planned to move onto the land in the spring.

In April 1948, brother Stanley married Shirley Nutter, a daughter of Fred's wife Molly from her previous marriage. Stan and Shirley had eight children before they divorced: Rita, Gary, Donna, Rick, Nola, Darrell, Stephen, and Debra. All are now married and have their own families.

To complicate the family tree even more, Stan subsequently remarried -- not once, but twice. His son Gary then wed the daughter of his second wife; later, son Rick married the daughter of wife number three. No wonder my brother was fond of the song

I'm My Own Grandpa.

In the spring of 1948, Marion and I sold our interest in the sawmill to Bill with an understanding that I would work for him whenever I could. The house on the property was not finished, so we moved in with Dad and Mom for a month until we could make the place livable. We were very happy with the property. A beautiful place, it consisted of 360 acres and one-half mile of lake shore.

We bought machinery, planted forty acres in grain and tilled a large garden. Marion, who always liked farming, was as happy as a lark. I never cared for the farming business myself, but certainly enjoyed the few years that we lived on this property. I wasn't pleased when the flooding of Ootsa Lake by Alcan forced us to leave. (More on that later.)

We really enjoyed that summer. Hugh and Myles Shelford bought property next to us; by now, they too were married, and their wives became good friends with Marion. It was also great for me to have Shelfords for neighbours again. Having Mohrs nearby was special, too; Elmer had married Monica Rist, and they became close friends as well.

In the fall of 1948, we lucked out by selling all our grain as well as some timothy seed. Having done considerable work on our house, we were prepared for winter.

With the arrival of hunting season, some of us decided to take a trip. We rented Elmer Mohr's boat and went to the west end of Ootsa to hunt geese and moose. The group consisted of my father-in-law, Mac Anderson, my four brothers-in-law (Clarence Anderson, Bill Bennett, Len Radley, and Dick Schrieber) and myself.

When we got to our destination, we located a large flock of geese, but they were on the other side of the river and too far away to bag with a shotgun. Yours truly was chosen to get one for dinner with my rifle. There was a large goose standing on a sandbar a short distance from the rest; I made a lucky shot and knocked his head off. I acted as if this good shooting was commonplace for me, but I'm sure I couldn't do it again.

Mac was elected cook, so he made a goose stew for dinner. It cooked for six hours but the meat was so tough we couldn't eat it and had to settle for the vegetables.

The following day, we cooked the goose stew for another eight hours, then tried it again. We had no luck; indeed, it seemed the more we chewed each piece, the bigger it got. That goose must have been a hundred years old. We finally chucked the entire mess.

Obviously, another goose stew was not on the menu, so we returned home. Though our hunting trip was not very successful, we did have a good time away from the stresses of work. The excursion also proved who among the group could cook, and if I remember correctly, the answer was no one. We all appreciated our wives' cooking when we returned.

The outing to West Ootsa was the only hunting trip we made as a family, and it is something to be remembered. Clarence and I are the only members of the group still living.

During the winter of 1948-49, we worked at Jacob Lund's. Fred Spicer and I ran the mill, and Jacob did the logging. Although Jacob was a good friend and neighbour, I must say he was a difficult man to work with. I wasn't sorry when the winter ended. We moved back to the farm and I worked at other mills in my spare time during the summer.

About this time, a relation of the Talbots came out from England and bought Bill Kerr's property. His name was Jim Sambridge. Jim helped us on the farm that summer, and the next year, his parents and sister came and settled on the property he'd bought. They remained in the community until the flooding of Ootsa Lake. Jim and his wife Gladys have a family and live in Langley, B.C. They remain friends with whom we correspond and visit occasionally.

Don Lang also came back from England that year. He'd lived at Ootsa as a child, but his father was killed in a logging accident and his step-mother took him to England. Don has remained here ever since, and is a respected member of the community. He loves to tell stories with lots of action, and our grandchildren listen in awe to these tales. Don and I prospected with Cap McNeil on several occasions, and he guided for me at different times. I always enjoyed working with him.

In the fall of the same year, we went back to work with Bill Bennett. Once again, I ran the mill and Bill did the logging. I had a young fellow working with me, Mike Eva, and he was always happy and willing to do anything. It proved to be a fun winter, and perhaps one of the most pleasant I ever spent logging or sawmilling. Even after we went our separate ways, Mike and I remained friends, though I'm sorry to say he passed away last year following a long fight with cancer.

In the spring of 1950, because Marion was expecting our second child, she stayed with her mother in town and I moved back to the farm. Nadine was born May 6. I brought them home the first day the ferry ran after the ice left Francois Lake.

I spent the summer as sawyer for Wistaria Sawmill. One day, a pin came loose in the set works, and while trying to fix it, my fingers were caught and painfully injured. There was silence for a moment when this happened, and when I turned to see what was going on, believe it or not, Arnold Dawson, my co-worker, was about to tap me on the head with the flat side of an axe. It didn't take me long to get free after that, but I left two fingernails in the gears. Arnold could not understand why I was so upset and called him a few sweet names. Vince Dawson, Arnold's brother, also worked at Wistaria Sawmill and was married to Phyllis Harrison, one of my school friends.

That fall, the Shelfords and I bought a timber sale north of Streatham. We hired Bud Andrews to put in a road, then set up two sawmills and built cabins for the winter. It proved to be a cold year, and as the cabins were built with green lumber, they were not very warm.

After moving home again in the spring of '51, we learned that Alcan had been granted a licence to flood Ootsa and its adjoining rivers and lakes to form the Nechako Reservoir. All people living on affected land, we were told, would have to move. There were many upset people and no one could get any definite answers from the company. We had many meetings with Alcan officials, but they used intimidation tactics to get us out.

In an effort to get a decent deal from Alcan, we eventually

organized a group and chose Cyril Shelford as our spokesman. Some residents didn't join and one by one sold their property to the company, but many of us kept up the fight and finally received reasonable settlements for our trouble.

Clearly, the times were a' changing. When Marion and I left for camp that fall, we moved everything out -- knowing our life on the farm was over.

Of course, these events had a dramatic impact on our lives. Yet change, no matter how unpleasant at the time, is seldom all bad. For example, when Alcan first began flooding Ootsa Lake, Don and Heddie Piper moved their family into the area -- and though no one knew it at the time, they would play an important role in the community.

Don served as attendant at the Skins Lake spillway, the facility through which Alcan releases water into the Nechako River system. Always active in both community development and entertainment, he and his wife became respected members of Ootsa Lake society. Furthermore, because they had children close in age to our own, they became good friends.

Because Don always used the phrase 'moons' to describe the passage of time, I wll say that he passed away several 'moons' ago. Though Heddie now lives in Burns Lake, we still see her frequently and she remains a treasured friend.

As for the Pipers' children, well, they dispersed across the province like seeds in the wind. We still see some of them from time to time, and I often think of their eldest boy, Wayne.

After not seeing Wayne for several years, we recently had the pleasure of meeting him again at a First of July celebration in Wistaria. This time, we were pleased to see his family with him.

"Alan, meet my daughter," he said to me with a grin when it came time to introduce his teenage girl. "She's sixteen years old and she knows everything." His comments made me think of myself at that age.

But of course, in 1951, all this was in the future -- and with the water rising in Ootsa Lake, that future looked uncertain at best. As a result, though we had a good winter in camp that year, we weren't very happy.

One day that winter, though, Paddy Carroll brought an old friend of his to visit. The fellow's name was John Carlson, and it somehow came out that he was looking for a partner in his Vancouver bowling alley. Much to my wife's dismay, I allowed myself to be talked into the partnership. We agreed to be in Vancouver by late May.

When we moved out of camp in 1952, we moved to a house at Ootsa Lake just long enough to dispose of our machinery and everything not needed in our new residence. We had an auction sale, packed a few things, and left Ootsa Lake. We were a sad family as we drove to Vancouver, not knowing whether luck or misfortune awaited us in B.C.'s largest city.

CHAPTER SEVEN
Our Year in Vancouver

U pon arrival in Vancouver, we went to John Carlson's house and met his family. He had four daughters at home: Ruth, Elsie, Esther, and Ellen. His wife had left him, and son George lived in the U.S. We were made at home and learned that although I'd be managing the alley, Ruth would be working with me. She was also the bookkeeper, and I must say an efficient one. I soon learned to respect her, and we became good friends.

The bowling alley, called The Kerrisdale Bowladrome, was located at 41st and West Boulevard. After I learned to manage the business, I never saw much of John.

Our house-hunting ended with the purchase of a place at 3422 West 36th Avenue. The location was a good one, as it was close to Dunbar Shopping Centre and only about 15 minutes from the bowling alley. We lived in a nice part of town, and I liked the work. Marion helped me clean the alleys each day and prepare them for opening at one p.m.

I suppose this was what most people would call a good life, but it was vastly different from the one to which we were accustomed. We missed the Ootsa area so much, and I couldn't help thinking of the lakes and mountains at home. Marion didn't like the city at all, but we had to tolerate it for the time being.

We made friends with a few families, and that helped ease our homesickness. We met Ray and Alma Pudsey, and Alma's parents, after arriving in Vancouver, and also managed to locate former Ootsa Lake residents Art and Polly Pelletier. We saw a lot of them during our time in Vancouver. We also met families that had formerly lived in Burns Lake.

Like most children, Reg and Nadine made friends easily and soon had many. Strangely, all the kids seemed to congregate in our yard, and I soon learned that we didn't mind them playing on the grass. Of course, we had the worst looking yard on the street, but the happiest kids. A professor from the University of British Columbia lived next door, and he was always complaining that I did not keep our yard as neat as his.

One day, I was working out front when Reg came to me crying. "Denny threw a rock at me," he said. Not paying much attention at the time, I responded by saying: "Well, punch him on the nose."

Denny, the rock-chucker, lived two doors away, and a few minutes later I heard a scream. Out the back door of Denny's house came Reg, really legging it. Denny's sister was two jumps behind him. They ran past me; she was so intent on catching Reg that she never saw me until I said: "What goes on here?"

Crying loudly, she skidded to a stop. "Reg just walked into our house and punched Denny in the nose," she sobbed.

"I'm sorry that happened," I noted, "but tell Denny he better not throw any more rocks at Reg."

Kids forget quickly, so it wasn't much of a surprise to see Reg and Denny playing together again the next day. We never heard any more about the dispute, so I suspect it was amicably resolved and then forgotten. They remained fast friends after that.

In the winter of 1953, Dad had a heart attack, so he and Mother came to stay with us. We enjoyed the time they spent with us. Unfortunately, even though Dad was eventually sent home, he never fully recovered.

One day toward spring I received a letter from Bill Richmond, the Game Warden in Burns Lake, informing me there was a guiding area available in Tweedsmuir Park. Bill, who knew how much I loved the park, wanted to know if I'd be interested in the territory.

At the time, a local electrician had offered me work anytime I

My partner in the bowling alley, John Carlson, with his daughters Esther, Elsie, Ellen, and Ruth. (Ruth also worked at the alley with me).

Nadine and Reg in front of our house at 3422 West 36th Avenue in Vancouver.

(Clockwise from upper left) Me, Millie, Stan, Mother, and my half-brother Fred Spicer.

Our former home. We lived here for 38 years.

wasn't needed at the bowling alley, so we had plenty to consider. Still, the possibility of getting a guiding territory in Tweedsmuir Park appealed to me; I thought a lot about my life, and after discussing Bill's letter at length with Marion, decided to move back to Ootsa Lake.

John, my partner in the alley, was upset when I told him. He thought I was crazy, and so did my parents. Yet Bill's offer of a guiding territory was the opportunity I'd been waiting for, and I knew Marion wasn't happy in the city.

The Mohr family had moved to Haney, so I knew their house at Streatham was vacant and for sale. Not long after making my decision, I phoned and asked if they'd rent it to me until I could sell my share in the bowling alley, at which time I would buy the place. They agreed, and we started making plans to move back.

Ray and Alma Pudsey also wanted to move out of the city, so they decided to move to Ootsa with us. Ray worked with me guiding for some time, and they have been here ever since.

Of course, during our year in Vancouver we'd accumulated a large amount of furniture and household goods, so I phoned Stanley and hired him to haul our stuff back to God's country in his truck. Ray, Alma, Marion, and I — accompanied by our respective families, and Stanley in the truck — made up quite a caravan as we left for Ootsa Lake.

Upon our return, it became obvious that things had changed in the Ootsa valley. Many of the old-timers had left, and the water level in Ootsa was rising rapidly. Alcan was building new roads above the expected high water mark, fully one hundred and forty-eight feet higher than the previous level of the lake.

Telephone lines also had to be moved. Telecommunications in the Ootsa valley at the time consisted of the old static line phones, and everyone shared the same line. Some people loved to listen in on conversations, which really made Dad angry.

Certain he knew one of the culprits, Dad decided to use the lady's name in vain during a telephone conversation. She immediately took the bait, and Dad responded by telling her that if she didn't like to hear her name used in such a manner, she should get the hell off the line. The fact that his assumption proved correct pleased him no end.

The telephone figured prominently in yet another bizarre incident involving my parents. One day, while Mother was sitting by the table during a thunder storm, lightning struck the phone, in the process splitting the wall paper and paralyzing her right side for a short time. The wall, cracked by the force of the explosion, was burned black but didn't ignite; the phone, of course, was completely ruined. Mother sustained perhaps the least damage, though only luck prevented her from being severely injured.

By this time, Mother had taken over the Wistaria Post Office, while Olaf Anderson performed the same duties in Streatham. It was at the latter facility that we received our mail for several years.

Clearly, many things had changed during our year in the big city. Yet the beautiful mountains and park remained the same, and still presented a wonderful picture from the hill at my parents' property.

Though unknown at the time, we'd live on the Mohr place for the next thirty-eight years. We'd raise our family there, and they'd all attend school in the Lakes District.

CHAPTER EIGHT
Back at Ootsa Lake and Tweedsmuir Park

Because there were two houses on the Mohrs place, we moved into one and the Pudseys took temporary possession of the other. Marion and I were pleased to be back in the Ootsa Lake valley. The water was rising in Ootsa Lake; this was not a pretty sight, but the mountains beyond were still as picturesque as ever.

Although I had seen some of Buster Harrison's guiding operation, it took some time to get organized and prepare for a guide-outfitting business. I had to learn a lot, but fortunately, Billy McNeil, the Van Tines, and Frank Henson were there to give advice. Ray and I had brought a cabin boat up from Vancouver with us, and soon started building a barge to haul horses across the lake. I bought some horses and pack gear from the McNeils and anyone else who had some available.

Slowly but surely, our business came together. Bill Richmond, the local game warden, was very helpful in getting the guide area and licences transferred to my name; by July 1, 1953, I was the licenced guide-outfitter in an area I had seen very little of. Though it hadn't been easy, our business (Tweedsmuir Park Guides and Outfitters) was finally a reality.

Yet on August 23, 1953 -- just when things were looking up -- bad news arrived. Dad passed away. This was also Reg's sixth birthday, but I doubt that he or any other member of the family had a happy day. Dad was buried on the Shelford Ranch next to Jack and Safie Shelford.

By winter we were ready to take out hunters, but we didn't have any. We spent the winter working in a sawmill, and on May 31, 1954, our second son was born. We named him Alan Neil, but to avoid confusion, he has been Neil ever since.

During the spring of 1954, Ray, I, and a neighbour decided to build a thirty-two foot cabin boat. Thanks in part to the experience I'd gained while helping Orald Harrison build boats at Fort St. James prior to the war, the finished product proved excellent. We used this craft for 16 years. My neighbour was a great help too, as he was a good carpenter. Unfortunately, a short time later he overturned in a small boat on Ootsa Lake and drowned.

During the next two years, I advertised my guiding services in magazines and hunting papers. To make ends meet and build up our equipment, we worked at different sawmills in the area. Then, on June 21, 1956, our second daughter -- Carol Anne -- was born. We now had six mouths to feed, so I had to keep my nose to the grindstone.

Reg's birthday in 1956 brought more sad news, however. That was the day Marion's father, Mac Anderson, passed away after a fight with cancer. He was only in his early sixties at the time, and should have had many good years left.

Despite these temporary setbacks, we now felt ready to explore Tweedsmuir Park. Established in 1936 to honour Canada's Governor-General, the park included more than 5,000 square miles of rugged wilderness. In 1937, Lord and Lady Tweedsmuir, with some of their family, made an extensive tour of the conservancy, lending their names to various islands and points. His Excellency, Lord Tweedsmuir, had this to say of the giant park bearing his name:

"I have traveled over Canada and have seen many wonderful things, but I have seen nothing more beautiful and more wonderful than the great park which British Columbia has done me the honour to call by my name. Its five thousand square miles contain some of the loveliest lakes, rivers, and mountains on the continent; it shows every variety of North American game except

86

mountain sheep; it provides a happy hunting ground for the sportsman, the fisherman, the naturalist, and the mountaineer. It is of historical interest, too, for there, Alexander Mackenzie completed his great journey to the Pacific. I write these lines to invite nature-lovers to this noble reserve and to assure them that they will not be disappointed."

Because Tweedsmuir was an area I'd always loved, I was anxious to ride over its old trails in search of campsites containing plenty of feed for our horses. On our first trips in, we saw plenty of wildlife, too; caribou and mountain goat were plentiful, and we sighted several grizzly. The south slope of Tweedsmuir Mountain was one of the big bears' favourite habitats; being an old burn, it had an abundance of huckleberries. On one trip, we counted nine grizzly on this slope.

A party of fishermen from California officially started us in guiding business. We took them in to Eutsuk in our new boat (its maiden voyage) and enjoyed excellent fishing. They returned for a hunting trip, and were very successful, so we had them (or at least some of them) as clients for many years. Ray was a good guide and lucky hunter, and they liked him. He had a knack for finding game, though it sometimes resulted in a bit more excitement than anticipated.

On one occasion, a hunter named Charlie Paine wounded a grizzly. It ran into thick scrub balsam, and Ray decided to go get it. To provide himself with some cover during this tricky operation, Ray put Charlie on a knoll and instructed him to keep a sharp eye out for the wounded bear. The bear, however, wasn't too keen on becoming a trophy; it hid in thick brush and charged Ray as soon as he came close. Fortunately, he shot and killed it at close range, but the experience left him badly shaken. I'm sure he went back to camp that night with bad stains in his underwear.

Another time, Ray arrived at camp late. After seeing our hunters to the cabin, he put the horses in the corral; yet just as he closed the gate, the animals suddenly spooked. Hearing a noise behind him, Ray turned to see a grizzly standing on its hind legs only a few feet away.

I was in the cabin at the time; hearing a mournful cry outside, I ran to the door. As I grabbed the portal's wooden latch, Ray hit it from the outside and pushed so hard that I couldn't release it. Finally, I gave a little extra pull, and Ray flew into the cabin, very pale but unscathed. As might be expected, he didn't venture far from his bunk the rest of the night -- though I noticed he put on clean underwear before retiring.

Though we all slept relatively soundly that night, dawn provided further proof that Ray -- and not the bear -- had been most shocked by their chance meeting at the corral. When I looked outside the next morning, the grizzly was ambling around about fifty yards from the cabin. The hunters were still in bed, so it was quite a circus when I asked if anyone wanted a crack at a grizzly. One hunter, who proved a little quicker than the rest, killed it with one shot from his .30 calibre rifle.

On our first trips in to the park, it was common to see between fifty and three hundred caribou in a herd. Indeed, these animals were so plentiful that they looked like a large carpet moving over the plateaus. Yet there hadn't always been a lot of them in the park; indeed, wolves nearly cleaned them out in the early 1940s. Fortunately, however, a wolf control program was brought in as an emergency measure, and by the early '50s, we again had nice herds of caribou in Tweedsmuir.

It's sad that most people today ignore these important facts. As I write this book, Tweedsmuir Park caribou are again in decline and wolf control is non-existent. I think it's a shame, personally; no one wants to see all the wolves killed, but it's important we keep a balance between predator and prey.

Think about it. Caribou, moose, mountain goat, deer, and mountain sheep are all vulnerable to predators (which include wolves, black bear, grizzly bear, coyotes, and man); on the other hand, if man is taken out of the equation, wolves and coyotes have only nature to contend with. Clearly, if we're to continue hunting, we must kill some predators to keep a balance. I have but one message for B.C.'s wildlife management branch: Wake up. Forget politics, you guys, and face the facts.

The boat we built in 1954 and used for many years.

RIGHT: Lord Tweedsmuir with a catch of rainbow trout.

Distinguished Visitors Here From England

Burns Lake and the Tweedsmuir Park district have as distinguished guests, Lord and Lady Tweedsmuir, who arrived last week from England on their first visit to Canada's largest scenic playground. Tweedsmuir Park was named after Lord Tweedsmuir's father, the first Lord Tweedsmuir, Governor-General of Canada from 1935 to 1940.

The British peer and his wife arrived at Prince George airport via CP Airlines last Thursday. They immediately boarded a Pacific Western Airlines plane for the Ootsa Lake area.

Lord and Lady Tweedsmuir plan to spend three weeks "roughing it" while they explore as much as they can and get in some big game hunting. They will spend two days at Kitimat and then go to Vancouver for a few days before returning east by train.

40, Tufton Court,
Westminster,
London, S.W.   1

2nd November, 1955.

My dear Alan,

      We have at least got back to Britain and got ourselves
sorted out. It's very hard to settle down to work again, as our minds
are always running back to B.C. and the wonderful times that we had with
you. We sit and look at the photographs almost every day. This, I am
afraid, is rather a sad story.   As you know, the photographs are all
in colour, and when you hold them up to the light, some of them are very
beautiful.   But, unfortunately, to be printed they have to be
considerably enlarged, and I have been told that only two or three of
them are clear enough to stand enlargement. However, we are going to
have some experiments made, and will let you know how we make out.

      I am going to take every opportunity that I can of
mentioning your name in quarters that would be useful to you from a
business point of view.   I am writing a series of articles in
publications in Britain, and will probably be doing the same in one or
two in Canada.

      It would have been quite impossible for our trip to
have been more fun. We really had a tremendous amount of good luck, The
moose is one example, and running into a bunch of goats on the last crag
at the end of a long day was another.   Also we had the most splendid
fishing weather. One of the things we enjoyed most about the   whole
trip was the companionship of yourself and your family, and of Ray and
Bill, and those of the Wistaria people that we met. You certainly did a
successful job of protecting us against publicity, for which we were
tremendously grateful.

      We are going to have the goat skin made into a little
rug, and hope to scrape up enough pennies together to have the caribou
head mounted, but the souvenirs that really matter are in our memories,
which will always remain with us.

      I expect it's pretty cold up at Wistaria now. Winter
has started in Britain, and the wild geese have arrived from the North,
which gives me something to look forward to at the weekends.

      My wife and I are ceaselessly scheming to see if we
cannot plan a repetition of our trip,and if we do manage to work out a
plan, we shall be letting you know pretty quick.

      This letter is to convey to you the very warmest thanks
of both of us, for the most wonderful holiday that we ever had in our
lives.   We shall be terribly grateful to get a line from you to hear
about things at Wistaria, as we both left a good deal of our hearts in
British Columbia.

      Al good wishes,

      Yours sincerely,

John Trueman

Alan Blackwell, Esq.,
P.O. Wistaria,   B.C.,
CANADA.

If you're a guide-outfitter or a hunter, it's difficult to get people in the Ministry of Environment's wildlife branch to listen to you. This is most unfortunate, because hunters and guide-outfitters often possess first-hand knowledge of wildlife populations and the preferred habitats of different species. I experienced this attitude many times in my thirty-eight years as a guide-outfitter. Don't get me wrong; I admire some of our wildlife biologists, though I don't think they can do a satisfactory job under the present system. In my opinion, wildlife management today is politically driven, and unless we all wake up, the province will soon face a shortage of game animals.

As might be expected, though, I wasn't too concerned about such things at the start of my guiding career. Indeed, I was most interested in trying to build my own business, which took some time and even more hard work.

By 1955, though, things began to shape up for us. That year, we had a three-week trip with the new Lord and Lady Tweedsmuir, the son and daughter-in-law of the British aristocrat after whom the park was named.

They were wonderful people who just wanted to be treated like anyone else. They didn't want us to hire any other help for the trip; instead, they assisted us with the work and insisted we simply call them "John and Priscilla." We had a good time together, and they wrote to Ray and I for several years. They even told Ray and I that the trip into Tweedsmuir Park was the best holiday they'd ever had. It's interesting to note, too, that the new Lord's description of the park was almost identical to that delivered by his father twenty years earlier.

In 1977, while on a trip to England, my son Reg and I had lunch with the Tweedsmuirs at the House of Lords in London. Our English relatives couldn't believe it.

"Oh, my God, you're posh," exclaimed one of my cousins. "Very few commoners get into the House of Lords." I responded to my cousin's comment by saying that as far as I could see, the Lord and Lady were very 'common' people.

Though 1955 proved to be a good year, we had even more success in years following. In 1957, we booked a large hunting party from Spokane. Cyril Shelford, accompanied by native guides Michelle Charlie and Donald Jack, took this group out for us.

I recall an incident on this trip that deserves mention. One of the party shot some ptarmigan, which he proceeded to pluck. Yet rather than simply bury the feathers or dispose of them by other means, he threw them into the camp fire.

This really upset Donald Jack, one of our Indian guides. "Don't do that," Donald said with complete sincerity, "you make it snow."

Everyone laughed, as there were only a few small clouds in the sky. Yet an hour later, much to the disbelief of all involved, it was snowing.

"I told you feathers on camp fire make snow," remarked Donald peevishly.

Despite the sudden snowfall, the members of this hunting party must have enjoyed themselves, because many of them came back to hunt with me in subsequent years. In fact, I visited two of them last summer; though both are well over eighty years old now, they're still very active. Not surprisingly, they always ask about Cyril and my two Indian guides.

Michelle Charlie worked with me for years, and during that time proved himself an honest and reliable guide. He's over ninety years old now and has lost his memory, but still manages to get around.

Michelle might not remember a lot about the times we spent together, but I've got enough memories of those years for the both of us.

One morning, Michelle left camp on horseback with a hunter named Gary from Georgia and instructions to meet me at another camp about 20 miles away. I figured they had plenty of time to hunt along the way, as I was on foot at the time; yet as it turned out, I reached camp long before them.

Afternoon passed into evening with still no sign of Michelle and his hunter. Then, as darkness began to fall, I heard a steady series of groans coming from the meadow. Low and behold, in came Michelle and Gary, with the latter slumped over his saddle in obvious pain.

Thinking the Georgian had suffered misfortune along the trail, I rushed up to the him. "Gary, are you hurt?" I enquired with genuine concern.

It was Michelle who spoke first. "Him soft ass," the Indian stated simply.

"No, Awm not hurt," Gary interjected defensively in his Georgia drawl, "but Ahm beat and ma' ass is so sore I couldn't touch it with a powda' puff."

Gary apparently wasn't kidding, because he spent the next day in bed -- much to Michelle's disgust. I learned later that after setting out from camp at 7 a.m. on the morning in question, they'd spotted a grizzly on another mountain and gone after it. They didn't bag the bear, but succeeded in riding more than thirty miles that day -- a long way for (as Michelle would say) a "soft ass."

Another native guide who proved his worth was Pat Edmund. Pat, who worked with me for a long time, had a good sense of humour and only one fault: a bad temper. He and I had several heated discussions over the years, but he was an excellent guide and we have remained good friends.

Once, Pat was guiding a young fellow named Mike from Wisconsin when they spotted a large grizzly in a meadow below. Because Pat hated these bears, he quickly suggested they go back and get me. "Alan likes to hunt grizzly," he said enthusiastically.

Mike wasn't buying any of it, though, and insisted they go after the bear immediately. Pat shuddered. "Okay," he said, "but I'm not sure my feet will let me."

They succeeded in shooting the bear, though, and Pat proceeded to skin it out -- except for the head and feet, which he left intact. He then tied the bundle on a pack horse and brought it back to camp.

Pat's name should have been Snow White, because he was still shuddering upon arrival.

"Pat," I said, sensing his discomfort, "I don't know why you're so afraid of a grizzly. There were two of you with large rifles. That bear never had a chance."

"I don't believe you," the Indian muttered, "and I'm certainly not going to waste any running time thinking about it."

There's no doubt the grizzly Mike and Pat killed was a big one. When Mike had the skin measured, it ranked sixth in the Boone and Crockett Club record book.

Pat, however, was unimpressed. "From now on," he said to me, "you grizzly hunter."

Pat's sense of humour always shone through. Once, when my old guide was driving gravel truck for the highways department on a job that employed six other men, the foreman told him he was going too fast. "You'd drive fast, too, if you were the only Indian on the crew and had six white mans chasing you," Pat replied.

I still see Pat Edmund often, and he always has a joking remark. Last summer, I was on my way to Burns Lake and saw him on the Francois Lake ferry. He had a grin on his face when he came over to talk.

"Well, Alan, it's just about time to go grizzly hunting again," he said.

"Pat, I'm getting too fat and lazy to climb those hills anymore," was my reply.

I expected an answer, and Pat didn't disappoint me. "You won't lose that belly, either, sitting behind that steering wheel," he noted with a smirk.

Pat wasn't the only 'character' I encountered during my years as a guide. Indeed, some of my clients were memorable individuals in their own right, and hunted with me for years.

Harry Saxton was one such man. He loved to tell stories, and some of them could be a little on the 'tall' side, if you get my drift.

Once, a few of us were caught in a bad wind on Ootsa; faced with high waves, we pulled into shore and spent the night in an old logging cabin. The place was a mess; we had to chase out the bush rats just to make it bearable. Yet it wasn't long before the stories started flowing.

"This reminds me of my early married days," Harry said thoughtfully, "My wife and I were living in a shack with lots of rats around. When it got dark, she would hold the light and I'd shoot rats with a .22 rifle.

"One night, I pulled the trigger and missed. I thought: 'Oh my

Harry Saxton in his story-telling pose.

My booth at the Portland Sport Show, February 1964.

God, I was pointing toward the chicken coop.' Well, I went out to see what had happened, and there were two dead chickens. That bullet had hit a nail, split in two, and killed both chickens."

As soon as Harry had finished this tale, his friend Randy Smith added one. "That reminds me of when I was first married," Randy stated wistfully. "The skunks were raising hell with our chickens. One cold night, we heard the chickens squawking, so I jumped out of bed and put on my long johns -- those kind with a flap on the back and the button that was always gone because you were in a hurry when you went to the outhouse. Well, anyway, I picked up my 12-gauge double-barreled shotgun, put a shell in both barrels, and headed for the chicken house.

"When I got there, sure enough, there was a skunk killing chickens. I pulled back both hammers on the gun and thought: 'If I miss with the first shot, I'll get him with the second.' But just as I took aim, my black lab dog stuck his nose on my bare ass. I pulled both triggers and killed every damn chicken in the place."

We had a good laugh, but later Harry got me alone and said: "The lying son of a bitch."

Harry Saxton passed on many moons ago, but his son-in-law, Jim Marquis, hunted with us for several years. Jim and his wife Jean are two very good friends, and when we see Jean, it's almost as if Harry has come back to life. She can imitate her father perfectly.

During my more than forty years as a guide, I heard many stories of the type Harry Saxton told, and some of them were almost unbelievable. Yet these 'tall tales' weren't necessarily the most memorable ones; sometimes, as they say, truth is stranger than fiction.

I doubt, for example, that I'll ever forget the time Charlie Paine mistook a bear for a pile of saddlery -- and lived to tell about it.

As mentioned earlier, Charlie -- who wore glasses to compensate for his poor eyesight -- was one of the first hunters we took into the park. After a long day in the saddle on one trip, we arrived at the cabin; Charlie went inside while I saw to the horses.

In good weather, we often left our horse tack outside. Yet on the evening in question, sensing that it might snow, I covered everything with a tarp.

Much later, after we'd retired for the night, Charlie felt the need to relieve himself. Not bothering to don his eyeglasses, he headed out the door and was gone for several minutes.

"Al," he suggested upon returning, "you'd better cover up your saddles, because it's snowing."

"I covered them," I said, but Charlie wouldn't take my word for it. He argued with me for what seemed like eternity, and even volunteered to cover the gear himself if I told where the tarp was kept. Tired and frustrated, I told him to go back to bed. He eventually took my advice, but not before cussing me out and saying I was an idiot for leaving my gear in the snow.

Next morning, I got up early and went outside. About an inch of snow had fallen during the night, and Charlie's foot prints were plainly visible. They ended about thirty feet from the cabin; sixty feet away were a set of grizzly tracks and a big ass print where the bear had sat and watched Charlie take his pee. My saddles and gear, covered with a tarp, were over by the corral.

I can picture the performance if Charlie, sans eyeglasses, had tried to cover that bear with a tarp.

Speaking of bears, this book wouldn't be complete without a word or two about my friend Oscar. He moved here with his family from California, loved fishing and hunting, and worked for me from time to time.

Oscar also loved dogs, and had two black labs. One weekend, my brother-in-law (Bill Durban) and Ray Pudsey went fishing with Oscar. The three of them took a boat to the mouth of Andrew Creek, where Oscar stayed fishing while Bill and Ray walked up the creek to try their luck in another spot. Oscar's two dogs ran on ahead.

About a mile from the boat, Bill and Ray saw two black animals running towards them. Thinking these were Oscar's dogs playing tag, they paid little attention. Yet as the animals came closer, Bill and Ray realized that although the animal in the lead was a dog, the one behind (and doing the chasing) was a bear.

As neither man had a rifle, they both took off for the boat at high speed -- long-legged Ray in the lead, short-legged Bill trying to keep up. When they arrived at their destination, they suddenly realized they were on the wrong side of the creek.

Each had to make a split-second decision, and did. Ray, being tall, tried to jump the creek but ended up in four feet of water. Bill -- thinking that Ray, as a guide, knew what to do -- followed the bigger man's lead and also leaped into the creek.

With the bear close behind, the dog went right to its master. Oscar, a big man with a loud voice, stepped back and started hitting that bear on the nose with his fishing rod. "Get out of here," he bellowed at the bruin, which by now was standing on its hind legs and waving its front ones in the air. "Get out of here, you black bastard, and leave my dog alone."

Faced with such stiff opposition, the bear took off into the woods. Soon after, Oscar's other dog came trotting in. Ray and Bill watched the entire show from the creek.

Oscar also had a float plane, and enjoyed taking people up for rides. To throw a little scare into them, he'd wait until airborne, then pull out a book entitled *How to Fly on Floats*.

Ray Pudsey left the business after a few years, but I carried on. Up to this point, we'd been using Buster Harrison's route up the mountain, but as it was getting very rough and rocky, I decided to cut a new trail. I only had it partially finished when the hunters arrived that fall; not knowing how they'd handle the ride, I sent three of them up the old trail with two other guides while I took another (a fellow named Dale) with me up the new trail.

On our way up the mountain, Dale and I scared up some grouse. One landed in a tree close to the trail, and just for fun, I took a hand axe off my belt and threw in the general direction of the bird. To my surprise, the axe cut the grouse's head clean off and knocked the decapitated carcass to the ground.

Without a word, I nonchalantly picked up the dead bird, tied it to my saddle, and continued on down the trail.

Upon arrival at camp, I unsaddled the horses while Dale went inside the cabin. As he entered, I heard him exclaim: "Don't fool with that guy when he has an axe in his hand."

Next day, Pat Edmund and I put a cigarette package at twenty feet, then tried to hit it with the axe. Neither of us found the mark; after that, I never tried to kill another grouse by this method when Dale was around.

During our years in the guiding business, we always treated our hunters well. They had cabins to sleep in, and Marion cooked for them at our home. However, I had to employ cooks for the pack-in hunts, and these hired hands came in different shapes and sizes.

Herb was a small man who had a hard time boiling water, but everyone ate what he cooked and seldom complained. He was our chef the time we took out two hunters from Italy and a pair from Kentucky.

One of the Americans was named Pete Wood, and he loved bugging the Italians, who had a poor sense of humour. Well, Herb cooked some macaroni one night, and it was awful -- just like glue. The two Eyeties left it on their plates, but after eating a good helping, Pete said: "Pass the macaroni, Herbie. Sure is good -- just like Mother used to make."

Joe and Tony, the two Italians, left the table grumbling, but Pete laughed his way through another plate full of Herb's macaroni.

Once, we hired a big Scandinavian by the name of Edwin as cook. Edwin could make a good meal, but had a bit of a temper. In fact, on one trip, I had to intervene to prevent him from throwing a client into Ootsa Lake.

You should have seen it. There was Edwin, holding the man by the collar of his coat and the seat of his pants, threatening to give him the old heave-ho. Of course, the hunter was yelling for help; he was about ready to fly when I got there and grounded him.

"Keep that S.O.B away from me," Edwin growled. I didn't have to say a word; the hunter gave Ed a wide berth after that.

There's little doubt that cooks like Herb and Edwin livened up camp life. Yet the true comedian of the lot was Howard Hunter, who weighed well over three hundred pounds. I flew him to the mountain by helicopter, but he had to walk between camps because -- to put it bluntly -- I couldn't find a horse that would carry him. Even the large one I provided just for this purpose lay down and refused to budge when Howard climbed aboard.

Howard, able to see the humour in everything, elected to hang on to the horse's tail and walk behind. One day, he traveled eight miles like this through the pouring rain; when we arrived at the cabin, the wool sweater he wore had stretched to his ankles. The big guy just stood and laughed and shook water all over. The hunters wanted to take him back to Los Angeles and make a comedian out of him.

Because Howard and I had not discussed his wages, I finally felt compelled to ask him how much he expected to earn per day.

"Well, don't pay me what I'm worth," he urged, "because I can't live on that."

Howard was, as always, just joking. In reality, he was an excellent cook and worth more than I paid him.

My hunting territory was encircled by the lakes and rivers, with one portage between Whitesail and Eutsuk lakes. This circle could be made with a flat-bottomed river boat; from my place at Streatham, we traveled west on Ootsa Lake, then up Whitesail Reach to Whitesail Lake. Fifteen miles farther along this body of water, we came to the start of our portage into Eutsuk.

The portage between Whitesail and Eutsuk measured almost two thousand feet, after which we put our boat back in the water and headed eastward along Eutsuk toward the Eutsuk River and Redfern Rapids (which could only be navigated by river boat). Next came Tetachuck Lake, a river by the same name, and then Euchu Lake. Halfway down Euchu Lake, we turned the bow of our boat in a westerly direction once more and entered Natalkuz Lake, before passing through Intata Reach and Intata Lake. Ootsa Reach led us directly into the east end of Ootsa Lake, thus bringing us full circle.

I first made this 'circle tour' with the help of Jim Morgan, an experienced river man and guide who was a big help to me in the early years. It's a wonderful trip with fabulous scenery, and -- having completed it several times over the years -- I highly recommend it.

During the late 1950s, we continued building up our guiding business. Then, in the fall of 1958, Marion realized she was pregnant again; on April 5 of the following year, we welcomed our third son, Michael, into the fold. It was also about this time that we finally realized why the babies kept arriving, and decided to do something about it. Michael proved to be the last addition to our family.

I bought another sawmill and some timber, and worked both when I had time away from guiding (which was usually in the winter months). We carried on in this manner for several years, until large forest companies like Eurocan Pulp and Paper moved into the country.

By the early 1960s, Reg was proving a big help around the place. He wrangled and loaded horses for me, and even guided some of our hunters. A few of his school friends also worked for me during the summer months, among them Lloyd Adams and Mike Collison. Gary Hainstock also helped us a lot. Later, my sons Neil and Mike also served their time in the guiding business.

I suspect if you asked any of them today what it was like working for me, they'd say: "He was a cranky S.O.B." Perhaps there were times when I seemed a bit owlly, but I doubt my mood resulted from their actions (or lack of them). On the whole, they proved good workers.

In February 1964 I took a booth in the Portland Boat and Sport Show, and it proved a wise decision. I booked a full house in 1964, and we repeated it in '65. From that year onward, Tweedsmuir Park Guides and Outfitters was booked solid every year.

By this time, of course, the country was changing. Eurocan Pulp and Paper's decision to establish logging operations in the area brought plenty new people to the community, and in 1969, we decided to put in a mobile home park to accommodate them. Before long, there were seventeen trailers on our property, and we were supplying electricity to them with a large power plant.

Because our power plant had a limited capacity, people who wanted to rent trailer pads from us were told even before they arrived that the use of electric stoves was taboo. Yet everyone knew the area would likely soon be serviced by B.C. Hydro, so they didn't pay much attention to our warnings. At the time, it didn't help that most trailers were equipped with electric stoves, either.

Well, as you might expect, there were more than a few people who tried to bend (if not break) the stove rule. What amazed me, though, was the fact that people actually thought they could get away with it.

The trailer park business almost drove Marion crazy. As soon as I'd leave the property, the owners of several trailers would turn on their electric stoves. This, of course, overloaded the power plant, causing it to slow down and belch black smoke, at which time other tenants would start phoning our house with questions about the plant.

To resolve the problem, Marion would have to run through the trailer court and locate those tenants using electric stoves. Believe it or not, some of them didn't have enough brains to realize what was happening. In frustration, I finally threatened to take the breakers out of their electrical panels.

With B.C. Hydro expected to start supplying the area with electricity, I decided to renew my electrical contractor's licence so that I could wire local houses. In the meantime, I worked for Strimbold Logging, the outfit contracted to build roads and clear the site for Eurocan's proposed camp at Andrew Bay on Ootsa Lake. Archie Strimbold owned the company, and I worked for him whenever I wasn't guiding; it was a good job, so I stuck with it until electrical service arrived in 1973.

Archie was a great guy to work for, and he always stopped by to chat with his employees. We could always tell when he was upset about something, though, because he'd arrive with a smile on his face. If he approached you wearing that distinctive smile, you knew you were in trouble.

Archie later sold his business and retired to ranching, but I understand that he still dabbles in logging from time to time. Interestingly enough, I recently heard that Cyril Shelford's son Kerry is managing the Strimbold ranch. I suppose it shouldn't come as too great a surprise; after all, this area has a habit of drawing people back to their roots.

CHAPTER NINE
Guiding and Electrical

The contract for building the power line to Ootsa Lake was granted to Combine Electric. The boss and one of his foremen stayed at our trailer park, so I became acquainted with them and the company's owner, Dan Dettweiller. I had successfully bid on contracts to wire many local homes, and my association with Combine enabled me to get a great deal on many of my supplies.

With work on the new power line underway, I hired additional help and was soon very busy wiring houses between Takysie Lake and Wistaria. My sons helped when they could, and Mike -- who took an electrical course in trade school -- proved to be a big help. Neil assisted when he could, but he was more interested in flying and left to pursue other interests.

Neil wasn't the only Blackwell interested in aircraft and flight; indeed, all of my three boys succeeded in getting their pilot's licences at one time or another. Apparently, their love of flight was contagious, because when Mike went for his licence, I also decided to get mine. Even one of my employees, an electrician named Ron Shively, took flight training with us. (Neil and Mike later acquired their commercial licences, but Reg, Ron, and I were content to remain private pilots.)

Somehow, in between the flying and electrical work, we managed to fit a couple weddings into our schedule. During 1974, we had two marriages in the family; on Feb. 2, Neil married Kathy

Jessee, and on April 13, Carol married Neil Endacott. Our family was growing up and leaving the fold.

As noted, our electrical business was going well, and I was lucky to have Ron working with me. He's a good electrician and was a big asset when I had guiding to do. Together, we wired many houses and businesses over the years; Ron, his wife Deb, and their family have been close friends ever since.

Tweedsmuir Park Guides and Outfitters was also doing quite well by the mid-1970s. We were getting better prices for our hunts, largely because Marion was now in camp. In fact, if the truth be known, it would have been difficult to make the guiding business a success without her. She was always there to help with the work, especially when that work involved horses. She loves these animals, and I wouldn't be surprised if they out-ranked me on her priority list.

Marion's talents as a cook were also an asset. The hunters, for example, loved her homemade bread and biscuits. There's little doubt that with good food and full stomachs, they were easier to please.

We also started doing a lot more hunting by boat, and as a result, our clients didn't end up quite so saddle sore. Sensing this *modus operandi* appealed to customers, I built a house boat for use on the lake. Propelled by an inboard/outboard motor, it was thirty-two feet long, twelve feet wide, and contained a 12'x16' living area. In addition to a propane stove and all the other facilities required for comfortable living, it had berths for six people.

Yet perhaps the house boat's most unique feature was its twelve foot deck. Located at the bow, this deck allowed us to transport three horses for use whenever and wherever land transport was required. For additional flexibility, we also towed our seventeen foot cabin boat and a fourteen foot aluminum skiff behind the house boat. Both could be accessed in a moment's notice.

The house boat proved to be an excellent piece of equipment. During hunting season, we could camp in a sheltered bay, hunt on foot, and still have horses to pack out game. So valuable was the boat that we used it for thirteen years, not only for hunting, but

RIGHT: Our house boat, which we used for 16 years.

BELOW: Hiking among the wild-flowers of Tweedsmuir Park.

Marion tying up the float plane on one of the many beautiful lakes in Tweedsmuir Park.

Tweedsmuir Park caribou swimming a lake during migration.

family pleasure trips.

Though the house boat was great, I still think hunting on horseback is wonderful. Nothing can quite replace a horse, which in my mind, plays an essential role throughout the North. In remote areas, for example, horses often provide the only available means of transportation.

Few guides or their hunters share my enthusiasm for horses these days. Most don't want to ride the animals, and even fewer want to take care of them. When we had hunters who liked to ride, though, I was always happy to take them.

Personally, I loved riding horseback through the mountains; it gave me plenty of time to enjoy the scenery. Believe me, if you haven't been above timber line in Tweedsmuir Park, you're really missing something. On a sunny day in August, when the wildflowers are in bloom, looking over Tweedsmuir Park from Michelle Mountain is the closest one can get to Paradise -- if not the Almighty Himself. I loved every minute I spent in the park, and wouldn't trade it for anything.

Unfortunately, I couldn't spend all my time up there. We had responsibilities back home, perhaps the least of which was the trailer park. We also operated a small store until Eurocan closed its operation at Andrew Bay. Marion took over the Streatham Post Office after Olaf Anderson passed away, and she kept the operation going until all the small postal outlets were closed.

The store was a profitable operation as long as the trailer park was full, but after Eurocan moved out of the country, many of our tenants moved away. As time went by, the number of trailers in our mobile home park dropped from seventeen to three. Soon after, we closed the store.

The entire experience was a bit frustrating. When we established the business, Eurocan assured us it was a good investment, but when they abandoned Ootsa Lake, we were on our own. It seems the time has come when you can't always rely on a man's word, only on his written agreement. It taught us a tough lesson, but we pulled through. We finally paid back the money borrowed to build the trailer park, and sold the property three years ago. Today, there are still three trailers in the facility.

In June 1979, the last member of our sizable flock flew the coop when Mike married Colleen Spence. They remained on our property, though, so we saw them often.

The 1970s and '80s also brought us several grandchildren. Ron and Nadine had two girls and a boy: Tanya (born October 1971), Melanie (August 1973), and Darren (March 15, 1976). Not to be out-done, Neil Endacott and our daughter Carol had two boys: Clint (born December 29, 1976) and Sean (born October 29, 1978). They later had a girl born October 25, 1984.

My son Reg and his wife Linda had two boys, Jason (born June 24, 1979) and Brad (born May 13, 1982).

Our Neil and wife Kathy didn't have any children. They later divorced, and I'm sorry to say that Kathy passed away after a fight with cancer. Neil remarried on September 13, 1988; he and wife Roanne have two children: Ryan (born April 12, 1989) and Carrie (born August 12, 1990).

In later years, Mike and Colleen also separated after having two boys, Justin (born July 13, 1981) and Jeremy (born January 9, 1984). Mike has since remarried, and the boys now live with him and his new wife Brenda, who had two daughters of her own (Jamie and Lindsay). Unfortunately, Jamie was killed in a tragic car accident in January 1996. She was sixteen years old at the time, a beautiful girl, and we all miss her very much. The accident has been difficult for the family.

As one might expect, the passage of time changed my businesses as well as my family. After Ron Shively received his Class B electrical certificate, he went into business for himself. I took less work as a result, and life slowed down considerably.

Marion, of course, kept busy. Somehow, though, she found time for an adventure or two of her own. In the early 1980s, for example, Gerry Schrieber and girlfriend Jude Robb from New Zealand asked Marion if she would join them in hiking the old Bella Coola trail. She accepted the invitation, but because she couldn't leave immediately, agreed to meet them part way.

Gerry and Jude started their trek from Tetachuck River, and Marion agreed to join them at Elgatcho, an old Indian village west of the Blackwater River. Mac and I flew Marion to Elgatcho Lake

Hauling our horses across Ootsa Lake in 1977.

Hauling horses in later years with our house boat.

and met Gerry and Jude there.

The three of them had a great hike along the Tanya Lakes, across the Dean River, and over the Rainbow Mountains. This was the same trail that brought the first settlers to Ootsa Lake in the early 1900s. Gerry and Jude hiked 150 miles, 100 of which came after Marion joined them. They saw caribou and had a bear scare, but did not see much game. They also encountered Indians fishing along the Tanya Lakes.

Mac and I picked Marion up in Bella Coola with the plane. Gerry and Jude, meanwhile, traveled by boat to Prince Rupert. The trip must have made an impression on the two visitors, because shortly after Jude went back to New Zealand, her brother Don booked a hunt with me. After bagging a bear and a nice moose here, he liked the area so well that he stayed with us for two years, during which time he helped with all our work.

We enjoyed having Don, Jude and their sister Sue visit us over the years. We formed a strong bond of friendship, and it was actually through Don and his family that Marion, Mac and I went to New Zealand in 1994.

All through this period, Marion and I continued to run the guiding business. However, in 1982, I took in two partners, Bob Neilson and Frank Reed. They were to work with me for five years and then buy my share.

The years with Bob and Frank were good; we worked hard, and spent many enjoyable times together. A fellow named Tommy O'Meara worked with us for a while, too, and he was a lot of fun. He provided plenty of laughs, and his wife Helen cooked us some fine meals.

Tommy hated horses, so we had several discussions over use the animals. It was fortunate that Bob, Frank, Tommy, and I all had airplanes, so we could easily move our supplies and guides from one location to another. From time to time, we also used commercial carriers to move hunters in and out of the territory.

During these years, we never suffered a shortage of good food. Frank's wife Marianne and Bob's wife Barbara are excellent cooks, so we enjoyed a veritable feast any time one of the wives was in camp.

Over the years, I also became involved in the Guide-Outfitters Association of B.C., and served as a member of the organization's executive on several occasions. In 1982, I was selected vice-president of GOABC, and the following year, took over as president -- a position I held until 1986.

I enjoyed representing the province's guide-outfitters and traveling throughout the province on their behalf. I made a lot of friends during my time on the executive, one of whom was Don Caldwell, the GOABC's executive director at the time. Marion and I have now been friends with Don and his wife Marg for many years, and enjoy their company.

While a member of the guide-outfitters' association, I was also honoured by my colleagues. Much to my surprise and embarrassment, B.C.'s guide-outfitters presented me with several awards during this period of my life, all of which are proudly displayed in my home -- even though I'm not sure I deserved them.

Not too many years ago, Bob Nelson finally bought out all the partners in Tweedsmuir Park Guide Outfitters. He is now sole owner of the operation, though I still guide for him occasionally. Marion never served as camp cook after Bob purchased the area, but rode in with the horses nearly every year -- an activity she really enjoys.

After selling my interest in Tweedsmuir Park Guides and Outfitters, I threw in with Reg and bought a small guiding territory formerly owned by Frank Henson (one of the area's early settlers.) Located to the east of my old stomping grounds in Tweedsmuir, it was good moose and bear hunting territory, and we kept it for several years. We used the house boat a lot in this area, and hauled in material for a cabin; indeed, the boat proved so useful that I wished I'd had it during my early years in the guiding business.

Despite changing guiding territories, we managed to retain some of our original clients. Indeed, when Kirk Neilson (our former partner's son) purchased the Henson territory from Reg and I two years ago, we still had some U.S. partners in the operation, former clients of mine whose association with me dated back to 1957. Now in their eighties, these men still enjoy the outdoors.

In February 1992, Marion and I moved and rented the old Mohr place out to another family until we sold it to Falko and Wendy Foersterling in August 1994. Though no longer officially associated with any guide-outfitting operation, I have done some work of this nature every year -- though less of it in the past two seasons.

During the thirty-eight years I owned Tweedsmuir Park Guides and Outfitters, I had a rewarding and enjoyable life. To tell you the truth, I can't think of any work more enjoyable. We had access to some of the best hunting, fishing, and beautiful scenery any where.

Exploring the lakes in Tweedsmuir Park by float plane was also a lot of fun -- at least for me. Marion never liked planes much, but we did a lot of flying into the park and even she learned to enjoy it. Though I tried to convince her to land the plane, she wouldn't so much as touch the controls.

I sold my plane a few years ago after experiencing some heart problems, but I miss having it. We also had to get rid of the house boat, but only because it became unseaworthy.

Marion and I kept our thirty-two foot river boat, which has a cabin and inboard/outboard motor. I built the craft myself, and this adds to the pleasure I get from using it.

We have made several pleasant trips in the river boat since its completion. We had a family trip planned for July 1, 1997 -- a week of fun and camping on Eutsuk Lake -- but had to cancel it due to high water. Perhaps we'll take the journey at a later date.

CHAPTER TEN
Travel

I've done a lot of traveling over the years. During my thirty-eight years in guiding, I made many trips to the United States, both for business and pleasure, and in the process acquired many good friends. In recent years, however, some of them have made that final journey to the Happy Hunting Grounds.

I have been fortunate, though, to travel beyond this continent. Over the years, I made several trips to Switzerland and Germany advertising my guiding service. More recently, Fred and I traveled to England, a trip that was proceeded by a visit there with Mother when she was ninety years old.

On her final trip to England, Mother needed a wheel chair at the airport. She tipped the attendant, mistakenly giving him a $50 bill instead of a $2. "Mom," I said, "you just gave that guy fifty bucks."

"I did not," she replied matter-of-factly. "I know what a $2 bill looks like."

I never said any more; after all, it was her money. But I could see that guy smiling as he walked away. I'll bet he thought: "There's a generous old lady."

In the spring of 1977, Marion and I — accompanied by our son Reg and his wife Linda — took a great trip to Europe. We first went to England and visited my relatives, then traveled by ship to Denmark, where we visited Marion's uncle, Andy Anderson.

Andy had lived in Alberta for several yeas, so he spoke English very well and was able to provide a running commentary on his country. For what he thought was a treat, he took us to Kentucky Fried Chicken. If only he'd realized that his guests were looking forward to Danish cuisine.

We enjoyed the meal and Andy's company, though. He reminded me a lot of Marion's father; some of their phraseology was identical.

When we left Denmark, we traveled by train to Hamburg, Germany, and there rented a car for the drive to Zurich, Switzerland. I knew a fellow in the Swiss city who'd hunted with me and been very successful. Much to my pleasure, he gave us a royal welcome and showed us a lot of the country. In addition to visiting The Kindly Club (a world-renowned watering hole in Zurich), we saw an annual event known as The Burning of the Winter. This celebration involved different tribes of horsemen riding around peaked up piles of straw that were eventually set on fire. It was an amazing display.

After an enjoyable time in Switzerland, we again boarded a train and traveled through Northern Italy to Monte Carlo and Southern France. This was a beautiful trip through some of the area I had been during the Second World War.

At Monte Carlo, we again rented a car and enjoyed several days' drive through France to Calais. Here, we boarded a large hovercraft and returned to England at Dover. We again visited some of my relatives and then returned home after a month of traveling. It was a fun trip, and Marion and I really treasure the time spent with Reg and Linda. I enjoyed seeing the reaction of Linda and Marion to some of the incidents and facilities we encountered; the public toilets in France proved a real surprise to both our wives.

Since selling our business, Marion and I have done even more traveling. In April and May 1994, we spent six weeks in New Zealand and Australia -- something I always wanted to do. We had friends in both countries, and as a result were shown all the impressive sights. Our son Mike went with us, and drove us around in a rented van. I even had the pleasure of a deer hunt in New Zealand, and there bagged a nice buck.

114

Yours Truly on my New Zealand deer hunt.

Enjoying the beaches of New Zealand.

Marion and I with friends Ray and Sandra Garroway in Australia.

Part of the Great Barrier Reef in Australia.

In Australia, we toured the Barrier Reef, and Mike went scuba diving. The colors and the amount of fish over the reef were amazing. We even visited crocodile farms and ate croc meat, which I must say was delicious. I suspect, though, that crocodiles also consider humans a delicacy, because we heard later that a staff member who'd shown us through the croc farm was killed by one of his 'livestock.' I don't know about you, but that doesn't top my list of Ways to Meet Your Maker.

All in all, though, the trip was wonderful, and I hope the Good Lord grants me time to repeat it, particularly the visit to New Zealand.

Though the holiday 'Down Under' was special, perhaps one of the most memorable trips of my life was taken in May 1995, when I visited France for the fiftieth anniversary of VE Day.

The ground work for this journey was laid during the winter of 1994-95, when I corresponded with my former battalion commander, General Ed Thomas. We wanted to do something to celebrate the fiftieth anniversary of the war's end in Europe, and hoped to be part of a contingent of Force members making the trip.

Initially, several veterans planned to go, but in the end, Ed Thomas and I were the only ones who went. In addition to laying wreaths at several cenotaphs in French towns liberated by The Force, we attended the dedication of a special memorial in Menton. My sons Reg and Neil also made the trip; Reg served as photographer and Neil was asked to carry the colours of the First Special Service Force -- an honour that pleased me immensely. The trip gave me an opportunity to show my sons where The Force's last battles took place, and where I'd fallen over the cliff during one assault. It was an emotional experience.

On our way home from Southern France, Neil, Reg and I spent time in England visiting relatives. My sons could only stay a few days, but I stuck around for two weeks and accompanied Fred Spicer home. I enjoyed visiting my English relatives -- just as I had during the war.

Later in 1995, Marion and I decided to attend a First Special Service Force reunion at St. Andrews, New Brunswick. To get there, we traveled across Canada with our pick-up truck and trailer. Our good friends and neighbours, Howard and Dorothy Hansen, accompanied us in their pick-up and camper. After attending the reunion, we went to southern Maine and visited some of my army buddies, then came home by way of the United States. On the return trip, we visited the Hansens' relatives in Wisconsin and Minnesota, as well as Marion's cousin whom she'd never met. We also spent time visiting and camping with friends. It was a wonderful trip and one we will always remember.

Because we'd made previous trips with Howard and Dorothy, we knew they'd be good company and a lot of fun. One of these trips was to Yukon and the Northwest Territories.

This trip to the Far North was taken by three couples: Howard and Dorothy, Glen and Betty from Portland, Oregon, and Marion and I. We visited many places (Telegraph Creek, Watson Lake, Whitehorse, and Dawson City) before driving the Dempster Highway to Inuvik. We all had a good time and saw some beautiful scenery. This is another trip I'd like to take again.

On our return, we drove from Dawson over to Fairbanks, then down to Anchorage by way of Denali Park. We took a trip into the park by bus, saw many animals, and got an excellent view of Mount McKinley (which was clear of cloud that day). At Anchorage, we camped for a few days, rested, and visited friends. We took a detour to Atlin, B.C., and then came home over the Cassiar Highway.

During those six weeks of travel and comradeship, we camped in many great spots and enjoyed some of the finest scenery North America has to offer. Strangely enough, despite the fact that Glen carried a small boat on his trailer, he never unloaded it -- even though we passed some great fishing lakes. I still haven't figured why he brought it.

We had a friend in Inuvik who married a beautiful Inuit girl, and she arranged for us to accompany her brothers on a whaling boat. Unfortunately, having left our motor home at the Mackenzie River (and our dog inside it), we had to decline what was probably the opportunity of a lifetime. We also missed out on a big musk ox

Crocodile farm in Australia. One of the employees was killed by a croc shortly after we left.

My son Mike Blackwell holding a baby croc. Its mouth was taped shut for this exercise.

VE Day celebration in Southern France, May 8, 1995. That's son Neil carrying the colours. Reg and I are on the far right.

Laying wreaths in Southern France, May 8, 1995.

1997 Army Reunion in Winnipeg. A few of my old friends are still living.

Yours Truly with a very special friend, Gerry Ceel. That's Gerry's wife Sue between us.

barbecue the following day.

I love to travel, but Marion is a home person. In April 1998, I hope to visit England with our two daughters, Nadine and Carol. They have not been to England before, and I will enjoy showing them all the interesting areas.

CHAPTER ELEVEN
Our Years of Gold Mining

When we returned from our trip to the Yukon in 1989, an old friend named Bill Glanville called and asked if I would be interested in placer gold mining. It seems that while I was away, our son Mike had flown Bill into a promising area north of Fort St. James by float plane, whereupon my long-time friend staked two placer claims.

Because both claims had good showings of the noble metal, we decided to mount a bit of an expedition into the area. Bill, Mike, and I hastily put together supplies and a tent, then flew into the area, landing on a small mountain lake a mile or so from our destination, Valleau Creek. After a taxing hike, we arrived at the wide, shallow stream along which Bill had staked his claims, and proceeded to pan some of the gravel bars and banks along it. Pleased with what we found, we staked four more claims in the area: one for Bill's wife Anne, one for Mike, and two for me. After cutting a rough centre line through these claims, we tracked back to the float plane and flew out, intending to return to the area later in the fall.

In early October, Bill, Anne, Marion, and I started looking for a trail to our gold properties along Valleau Creek. We had maps that showed us we should start on an old road that previously linked Fort St. James with the gold rush community of Germansen Landing. After traveling a few miles along this nearly abandoned

Passing Klawli Lake on our way to stake claims on Valleau Creek, September 19, 1989.

route, we saw a cabin with smoke coming from its chimney. Upon arrival at the rustic dwelling, we were welcomed by its owners, an elderly couple named Oscar and Edith Sweeder.

Though they have since become good friends, the Sweeders at first tried to discourage us from traveling any further into the isolated country beyond their home. I suspect that because they didn't know us from Adam, and couldn't be one hundred per cent certain of our intentions, this old pioneer couple didn't know if they could trust us along what we later learned was part of their trap line.

We finally made a breakthrough of sorts, however. "So you're a Blackwell," noted Oscar well into the conversation. "Now, you wouldn't happen to be related to Neil Blackwell of Ootsa Lake, would you?"

When I responded that Neil was my son, the entire tone of our conversation with the Sweeders changed. It seems that Oscar and Neil had once worked together for Bond Brothers Logging, during which time they'd developed a mutual respect for each other's abilities and character. Apparently, Oscar decided that if Marion and I had produced Neil, we couldn't be all bad.

In this way, thanks largely to Neil's good reputation, we earned Oscar's trust. It proved invaluable in the months, weeks, and years ahead, as the old trapper shared both his knowledge of the area and his cabins with us -- both of which were very much appreciated. In fact, I doubt that we'd have found the road in to Valleau Creek without his help.

On October 14, Oscar led us to the shallow but fast-flowing Klawli River, where we thought we found a suitable spot to cross. Oscar had a cabin here, so we moved in and decided to start work on a bridge.

For the next two days, we built bridge piers. Marion and Anne packed hundreds of rocks and piled them in frames constructed by Bill and I. On October 17, we cut and skidded the trees with a chain saw winch, and on October 18 and 19, finished the structure. The following day, we headed home, thinking everything was in order for the next year's crossing.

In late November, Bill and I went to Fort St. James and obtained permits from the B.C. Forest Service to cut timber for additional bridges and cabins. In January, with heavy snow blanketing the country, we went to Prince George for the necessary mining permits.

It was decided that later in the winter, we'd travel to Valleau by snowmobile, taking as many supplies as possible with us. During February, Anne and Marion canned moose meat for camp.

Finally, the big day arrived, and we left for our claims. We got to Twelve Mile on February 24, but finding the Sweeders' cabin empty, we returned home and started out again on March 6, 1990. Our plan was to locate a trail and pack a runway on Wudtsi Lake so that Neil could fly in materials and supplies with his versatile Otter aircraft.

We took our motor home to the trail head (where it served as a base camp), and from March 6 to March 11, freighted supplies to Twelve Mile with sloops. On March 12, Oscar came with us and we moved to Klawli cabin, which from this point on served as a new base of operations.

The next day, March 13, Oscar took off on snowshoes to scout trail. Bill and Oscar got to Grizzly cabin, and I joined them the next day. It was -20 degrees Fahrenheit.

Even with Oscar helping us, it took twenty days to get everything to Valleau. We then packed a runway and went home.

Bill had hurt his eye on March 8 and had to be in Vancouver on April 7, so it was decided that a couple of us would snowmobile back in to Valleau. Neil would then bring Bill with him when he flew in materials for camp.

On April 4, we made sloops and prepared for another trip back to the claims. Bill went to Vancouver on April 7; Anne, Marion, and I left for Wudtsi Lake early the following day. We took our time going in, and we had a good trip.

On April 15 at eight a.m., Neil arrived with Bill, Rex, and supplies. We started hauling the freight immediately, and had everything to Valleau by one-thirty p.m.

By now, however, we were getting a little anxious, as it was growing warmer by the day. The snow was thawing fast; though we left Valleau at 8:30 a.m. April 16, we ended up stuck on a hill and didn't get to Sweeders' cabin on the east side of the Klawli River until 2 p.m. Here we had to stay, hoping our trail through the snow would freeze over night. By six p.m., we discovered two feet of water over our tracks on the river. We'd made it over the Klawli just in time.

We stayed at Twelve Mile with Oscar on April 21, fixed the motor mounts on Bill's snow machine, had breakfast, and then left. Because we were breaking trail, it was a tough trip; still, we managed to reach the motor home a little after noon, and drove back to Ootsa.

In retrospect, I suppose we were lucky to have made the trip with so little trouble. A day later leaving Valleau, and we'd have been stuck on the wrong side of the Klawli River.

During high water in June 1990, Bill flew over the Klawli River and had a look at our bridge. All our work had been for naught; there was no sign of the structure. Apparently, it had been washed out, even though we built it five feet above low water. We were now back to square one.

On July 6, we loaded trucks, picked up Oscar in Vanderhoof,

Mining partner Bill Glanville and I standing beside Central Mountain Air's turbo Otter on Wudtsi Lake, approximately two miles east of our placer claims. In winter, the plane (equipped with skis) landed on the ice with our supplies; in summer, it did the job on floats.

and reached the end of the Sylvester Creek logging road at eight p.m. After setting up our tents, we retired for the night -- only to be awakened at 6:30 a.m. by the steady buzz of mosquitoes. It was lucky that we had good tents with thick screens, because the bugs were hungry.

We picked up camp and left early for Twelve Mile cabin. Oscar agreed to go with us and build an all-terrain vehicle road to Valleau. We were able to follow an old road part way to the claims, but it had to be cleared and there were bridges to be built over several creeks.

Clearing trail and fighting bugs, we arrived at Twelve Mile cabin by four p.m. July 7. We worked the rest of the day on Oscar's 420 John Deere crawler, as he was taking it to help build the road. At noon on July 8, we were on our way again; after traveling to Possum Creek (where a bridge was needed) we set up camp.

We skidded logs and built the necessary bridge by early afternoon July 10, then continued on to Klawli cabin, where we stayed two days. Oscar found a shallow ford on July 11 at a place where the river split into three channels; we crossed the Klawli without too much difficulty, and on the same day managed to get trail built to the foot of a hill across from the Klawli cabin.

The next day, we moved camp to Mica Creek, built a bridge, and got the crawler and machines across. By July 15, we were within a mile of Grizzly cabin. Here, we started back to get more supplies.

We helped Oscar with the roof on the Klawli cabin on July 16, and also repaired some mud holes in the trail. On July 17, we made our way home, thankful to get away from the bugs for a few days.

On July 26, we left home at 6:30 a.m. bound for bug country once more. Marion and I picked up Oscar, arriving at the beginning of the trail by noon and making it to Twelve Mile that same day. On July 27, we went on to Grizzly camp, where the flies were terrible. I don't think I've ever seen black flies as bad as they were there. Mosquitoes are bad at the Whitesail-Eutsuk portage, but at Grizzly cabin, we were set upon by what seemed like every blood-sucking insect on the planet. We all wore head nets, but it was difficult to eat any lunch. Our screened-in tents were a welcome sight when we got to the end of the trail at 5:30 p.m.

On July 28 and 29, we worked on trail and made it to Tsaydaychi Lake. We thought this was tough going, but the next few days proved otherwise. Along the north shore it was steep and a lot of side cuts had to be made through plenty of rock.

After fighting this section of trail for three days, a track broke on the crawler. Oscar and I headed back to Twelve Mile late one afternoon, where the old trapper kept spare parts. While we were gone, Bill took the crawler track apart and worked on road.

Oscar and I returned on August 2, and by evening everything was ready to go.

The following day, we got to the west end of the Tsaydaychi and set up camp -- just in time to receive company. People from

Fernie had flown in to a cabin on the south side of the lake, had seen us working, and came over to see what was going on. We had a nice visit.

On August 4 and 5, we moved camp closer to Wudtsi and built road as far as the summit between the two lakes. On August 6, it was raining and hailing -- which, while creating minor discomfort, at least kept the bugs at bay. Marion and I went back to Klawli cabin for more gas, and by August 8, we all reached the Wudtsi cabin. After stowing everything there, we headed for home and a few days of R & R.

On August 16, having loaded Bill's trommel frame (a piece of mining equipment) on a trailer the previous day, we were on our way again. Burdened by equipment, we didn't reach the Klawli cabin until 8:30 p.m.

We got a poor start on August 17, as my ATV sustained a flat tire after crossing the Klawli River. We didn't get away from this bug-infested spot until late morning, and then had a tough trip all the way to Wudtsi. At 11 p.m. that night, we left Bill's trailer in a mud hole about a mile from the cabin. We were all very tired when we finally reached camp.

The next day, Bill and I went back, picked up his trailer and continued working our way along Wudtsi Lake. Oscar dug out his favourite fishing gear, so we had fresh trout and Rocky Mountain white fish to eat. We thankfully reached the trail to Valleau on August 22, 1990.

On August 23, it rained hard all day and we stayed in camp. The following day, however, we moved everything to Valleau.

It was at this point that we suffered some more tough luck. On the trip to Valleau, Marion fell off her all-terrain vehicle and broke a leg. Fortunately, we had two-way radio communication with the outside world, and were able to call for help. Our son Mike and his wife Brenda flew in to Wudtsi on August 25 and took Marion out to the doctor.

While Bill moved across the river and dug some test holes, I started doing assessment work on our claims. On August 26 and 27, we cleared a walking trail for about two kilometres up the creek, then came back and set up an Alaskan sawmill and cut a few boards.

I went back on August 29 and picked up the rest of our stuff. I returned by 8:30 p.m. and was promptly serenaded by a pack of howling wolves. Because the creatures sounded close, we tied up the dog; it proved a fortuitous decision, because they came in very close that night.

From August 30 to September 5, we skidded logs, cut cants and lumber, excavated, and started building the cabin. We tried to dig a cellar, but abandoned the idea after hitting water at a depth of two feet. We also hauled limbs and filled some mud holes.

Bill and I had to go to Prince George to report our assessment work, so Mike brought Rex in to stay with Anne while we were away. We left September 5 and were back by 8:30 p.m. two days later. Mike and Rex stayed over and gave us a hand building the cabin on Sept. 8 and 9. They left at six p.m, but not before we were able to saw and assemble four levels of cabin logs

By September 15, we had the cabin walls up to twelve rounds, and five days later, got the rafters up and a doorway cut. Marion came back on the plane with Neil in the afternoon, and we moved into the cabin the following day -- even though it lacked a door. The structure had taken us a mere three weeks to build.

While Bill and I were working on the cabin, Anne had been hauling, splitting, and piling fire wood. With a sizable pile of fuel thus accumulated, we all devoted our energies to finishing the cabin. On September 24, after we completed the cabin roof, sheeted the ceiling, and set up the wood stove, Bill started on the door. Marion and I put the time to good use by starting on a storage shed, while Anne kept busy cleaning up.

By September 28, we had the shed finished and both windows and a door in the cabin. We also fashioned heavy wooden shutters for the doorway and windows, as these were needed to keep out marauding bears.

For the rest of the month, we did a little mining and testing. Anne and Marion washed clothes, cleaned up, and put things away. Marion and I had to be home by October 1, so Mike flew in on September 29, stayed overnight and helped with some sampling before taking Marion and I out with him in the afternoon.

Finding and building a trail to our claims along Valleau.

Our first camp at Valleau, August 23, 1990.

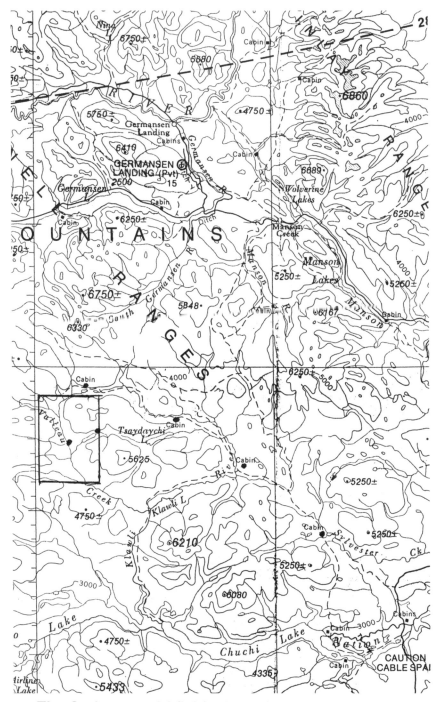

The Omineca gold fields, including Valleau Creek.

I'm told that after we left, the weather turned bad. By ten a.m. October 1, Bill reported four inches of snow. He and Anne built bunks in the cabin and an outdoor toilet during the next two days, but when it started snowing again on October 4, they packed up and left camp at three p.m. They had a tough trip out, with the ATVs churning through five or six inches of snow, but they made it back to civilization without too much trouble.

Marion and I had left our four-wheelers at Wudtsi Lake, intending to go back in on October 8 and join Bill and Anne for the trip out. Instead, Bill and I flew in on October 8 and brought the two machines out. By this time, the weather was better and we came out with no trouble.

Back at home for the winter, we now looked forward to the next year. We had a decent road built and a nice, comfortable cabin to stay in. Now to find the gold!

By July 1991, we were back at Valleau. Bill had brought his small crawler and a backhoe, so we set up the trommel and fed gold-bearing river gravel into it with the loader and backhoe. This required considerable preparatory work, as we had to construct settling ponds and wingdams to prevent silt from flowing into the river. However, we were pleased with the amount of gold we found, which included a few nice nuggets.

During the summer, we did assessment work on our claims and tested other areas. Much to our pleasure, we found showings of gold on every claim; indeed, when we finally left Valleau in September, we'd had a successful year.

We had reasonable success again in 1992 and '93, and certainly enjoyed the time we spent at Valleau. One winter, I made a float of Styrofoam. After covering it with plywood and Fiberglas, I put skis under it and pulled it into Wudtsi Lake with my snowmobile. The following summer, the float served as both a dock and (after we attached a motor to its stern) a raft that could be used for trolling.

As we learned earlier, there were beautiful trout, dolly varden, and white fish in Wudtsi; occasionally, we'd take time off from mining and go angling. It proved a satisfying diversion, and provided us with several good feasts of fresh fish. I don't think I have ever seen trout with such red meat.

During our years of mining, we had a few visitors to the cabin and they all had fun fishing Wudtsi Lake. The Glanvilles' daughter and her husband spent a few days with us once, and they caught some nice trout. Oscar Sweeder also brought his grandson to fish, and the lad was really excited with his catch.

Late in the summer of 1993, we found we weren't reclaiming enough gold in relation to the amount of equipment being used. With our backhoe being too small to move the large rocks and environmental regulations growing more stringent, Bill decided to forego use of large, motorized equipment. It was decided that we'd each work on our own with small dredges, and we operated in this manner for the remainder of '93. When we left Valleau at the end of the season, Bill took his backhoe and small crawler out with him.

When we went back to Valleau in July '94, Anne didn't accompany us. Bill worked his claims, while Marion and I worked mine. We carried on this way all summer, and were quite pleased with the results obtained prior to leaving for Prince George to record our assessment work.

The future looked bright when we left for P.G., but -- like the weather at Valleau -- changed all too quickly. On our way back to the claim on September 8, I had a bit of bad luck. About half way to the cabin, one front wheel of my ATV hooked a stump; in the ensuing scramble, I was thrown against a tree.

At the time, we didn't think the accident was a serious one. Marion helped me get up, and together, we got my machine and trailer back on the trail. We then carried on to Valleau as if nothing had happened; although I was very tired and sore, and suffering from a slight headache, I didn't think I was seriously hurt.

My diagnosis proved incorrect. When we arrived at camp, we unloaded both trailers and put the machines away, then headed for the cabin. Yet as I reached the top step leading to our porch, something happened; as I recalled later, it was like being hit on the head with something. Suddenly, I found myself laying on the porch, unable to get up.

Bill and Marion helped me into the cabin and it was then that I

Building our cabin at Valleau.

Cutting cabin logs with an Alaskan sawmill.

The cabin — finished after three weeks of hard work.

Bill's wife Anne inside our comfortable cabin — a welcome change after a summer of tenting.

Bill and I dredging for gold in Valleau Creek, 1993.

The reward for our efforts — gold.

A summer scene from the south side of Valleau Creek.

A winter scene.

realized my right side was partially paralyzed. It was a scary sensation; although the left side of my body felt normal, the right side of my face was numb, as well as my right arm and leg.

I sat on a chair while Marion made supper and Bill put things away. When I tried to eat, I couldn't find my mouth with a fork; this was a weird feeling, but I finally managed to eat and get into bed. Next morning, I was able to walk around with the help of a stick, but was in bad shape. With a lot of persuasion from Bill and my forceful wife, I agreed to call Neil on the radio phone and ask that he airlift me to the hospital in Smithers.

Neil came in next morning to Wudtsi Lake, and with help from Marion and Bill, I managed to ride my ATV from camp to the lake. Our grandson Jason and nephew Stewart came in with Neil and rode our vehicles out, so Marion was able to come with me on the plane.

In Smithers hospital, they did several tests and took X-rays, but couldn't confirm the problem. After a few days, I was sent to Terrace for a CAT scan, which confirmed the worst: I'd suffered a stroke.

Fortunately, by this time I was starting to recover the use of my arm and leg. Several people told me I should count my blessings, because the stroke had not affected my speech and my body was showing signs of recovery.

That was nearly three years ago, though, and I have not fully recovered. I can, however, still do light work and walk short distances. I have seen several doctors over the past two years, and they all tell me the same thing: Though I'm lucky to be alive and as well as I am, my condition will not likely improve further.

Needless to say, the accident put an end to my career as a placer miner. I'm disappointed that I can no longer go in to Valleau, as digging gold was a nice hobby (and sometimes a rewarding one). I miss it a lot, but have to accept the fact that my days of running a gold dredge are over.

Bill and I have since sold our placer claims and cabin to a young man from Burns Lake. He and a friend have worked the claims each year, and are apparently recovering a fair amount of gold.

Thinking back on the years we spent in the Valleau country, I cannot give enough thanks to Oscar and Edie Sweeder for the help and friendship they gave us. They still trap the area in the winter, despite the fact that both are well past retirement age. What a remarkable couple.

I talked with Edie in May 1997, and learned that Oscar was about to celebrate his eightieth birthday. At the time, he was working alone along the Klawli, far from civilization and all its conveniences. Apparently, the Klawli had changed its course that spring and was flooding his cabin; he took it upon himself to move the dwelling to higher ground -- a task that would normally require several ordinary men working in concert. But then again, as I said, Oscar is no 'ordinary' man.

CHAPTER TWELVE
Forced Retirement

It is with regret that I can no longer do much physical work. I miss gold mining very much, but my balance is bad and I have lost some strength in my right arm and leg. There's little doubt that long rides on All-Terrain Vehicles are out for me.

Despite my condition, I still manage to do a little guiding, though most from a vehicle or boat. Fortunately for me, the majority of my clients are hunters in their eighties, men I've known for thirty years, and they don't run too fast, either. Yet regardless of the circumstances, I still enjoy the companionship of these men who still love the wilderness and don't get upset if they fail to bring home an animal. This is my kind of hunting.

Believe me, it's difficult to retire after leading an active life. I have made up my mind, however, to enjoy every day to the fullest and look at the green side of the grass as long as possible. I read a variety of books, including the Bible, as well as newspapers and magazines; indeed, I spend several hours each day with my nose in a book. We also play a lot of card games; Marion and I usually enjoy a few hands of crib at breakfast time, and often play canasta with family and friends. This is a card-playing community.

Last year, when I decided to write about my life at Ootsa Lake, I took the challenge and bought a computer. Though completely computer illiterate when I started using the machine, I find I'm now mastering things I thought impossible six months ago.

Writing has given me much pleasure, and I find that time passes all too quickly. Indeed, although I don't work as hard as I once did, there still doesn't seem to be enough time in each day for all my chores.

I'm sure Marion is enjoying our retirement, as she now spends a great deal of time with her horses. I do believe they have top priority around our household. She is now talking about getting some chickens, too. I suppose that as long as she isn't making noises about buying sheep, I'll go along with her plans.

In addition to her horses, Marion loves her grandchildren and spends a lot of her time entertaining them. Most of them love to come and ride the horses or go for rides in a cart or sleigh.

As long as our health holds out, Marion and I have great potential for having fun. We plan to spend time traveling with our fifth wheel trailer, and more time cruising the lakes in our boat.

Marion's family, the Andersons, have a reunion every two years, and these events have proven to be a lot of fun. Because members of the Anderson family live in communities ranging from the U.S. to Alberta and B.C, get-togethers of this sort have to date been held in Brooks (Alberta), Sorrento (B.C.), and Burns Lake. In 1998, the traditional family get-together will be held August 2-4 in Revelstoke.

We've attended all these reunions, and enjoyed meeting all the relatives -- many of whom we had never seen before. Personally, I think family reunions are wonderful. The Blackwell family have had a few, but I hope we can have more.

September 6, 1996, Marion and I celebrated our fiftieth wedding anniversary. Our children arranged a wonderful party for us at the Ootsa Lake Bible Camp, which has great cooking facilities and several nice cabins. Though they contacted friends and relatives from throughout B.C. and the U.S., no one gave away the secret; as a result, the event came as a complete surprise to us.

It was great to see so many friends and relatives turn out to help celebrate our fifty years of married life. Our children and grandchildren put on several skits and told many humorous stories about us -- much to our embarrassment and the delight of our guests. I'm not ashamed to say that more than a few people shed tears on this day, myself among them.

Marion with her No. 1 love, Tassen.

Our granddaughter Tanya on Tassen.

Our family a few years ago.

Pondosy Bay, Eutsuk Lake.

Our children also sent us on a trip by train to Edmonton. It included three days at the Fantasy Land Hotel, and thanks to them, our first night was spent in the hotel's bridal suite with flowers, champagne, and a hot tub. Marion was provided with a nice night gown for the occasion, while my son Reg and his wife Linda gave me G-string shorts. I was unable to get a picture of Marion, but when I saw a picture of me in my special shorts, it was easy to understand why she says: "People don't need sex after sixty."

We did have a great trip and it's one we'll always remember.

As mentioned earlier, we do plenty of traveling. My army unit, the First Special Service Force Association, holds reunions every year, alternating between Canada and the United States. We have attended several and really had a good time meeting old buddies and their families. I would like to attend every year, but some are held in such far away places as Georgia and Florida. That's just too far to travel.

Marion and I are fortunate to have our children and their families close enough to visit often, and thus we have the opportunity to enjoy our grandchildren. I find I have more tolerance with them than I did with my own kids. This is probably because I have less stress and fewer financial problems now than when Marion and I raised our family. In fact, I distinctly remember a local lad saying to my son Reg: "Your Dad is surely a cranky S.O.B." I probably was, too. I'm a real pussycat now, however. Just ask my wife!

It's interesting to observe our children raising their families and see that they face many of the same problems we did. However, I think they have a more difficult time as parents, and it's due at least in part to the lax society of today. There is very little discipline in many homes, and perhaps even less in our schools. Many children do not respect any kind of authority, and this makes it difficult for parents who wish to raise their children with a little discipline.

Last November, for the first time in ten years, I was free from being a school board trustee. Although I enjoyed my years of public service, seeing what teachers put up with from some students was a real eye-opener. I do not wish to brand all students as bad, as only a few cause problems, but it is obvious that today's school system lacks discipline and the policies needed to enforce it.

Once, after a student and his parents came before the board on a disciplinary matter, I found myself in trouble for making such a remark. "It would be smart," I said at the time, "to again allow the paddle. Use it on the parents first, and then the student." While I admit this comment was not politically correct, I do believe the suggested action might prove useful in many situations.

One of the things that really bothers me these days is the corrupt language used by so many young people. When I was a student, using such language was all but unheard of. In fact, the most foul comments I've ever heard (and this includes all the stuff I was subjected to during five years of army life) came from a group of female high school students not that long ago.

This is sad, and I hate to think what the future will be like if we, as a society, don't start stressing better morals and manners. Last week, a fifty-year-old man told me that he's heard "F--- Y--" from more young people in the last year than from all the people his age in his lifetime. I hope things change soon.

Yet if the future seems bleak to us old folks, I can imagine what it must seem like to members of the younger generation. They have plenty to worry about, too.

For example, it seems that in this day and age, no one's job is secure -- even if they work for a large company. Case in point: I believe I mentioned early in my book that our son Mike worked for Alcan Aluminum. Not so anymore; a few months ago, as a result of down-sizing, he and one of his supervisors were notified that their services were no longer required. Mike had worked for the company for a decade.

Fortunately, Mike is a man of many talents. Being an experienced commercial pilot, he never spent any time unemployed after Alcan down-sized its workforce in this area. He is now flying for Inland Air, a regional airline operating out of Prince Rupert.

Yet Mike is perhaps one of the lucky ones. There are plenty of other young people in similar or worse situations, many of them without any skills to fall back on. For these individuals, I can only hope that economic and social conditions improve.

Although I still worry about our schools and students, I don't miss the two or three trips I took each month to board meetings. I see some of the present trustees every week, so I keep up to date on school activities. After hearing many of their problems, I'm pleased to no longer be involved.

As I get closer to the conclusion of this book, I feel compelled to mention the names of some of the super characters I have been privileged to meet in my life in the Ootsa Lake valley. The list includes Jack Shelford (who lectured me, along with his sons, on how to pick a good wife); Arthur Shelford (who helped me with my correspondence and spoke French with an English accent); Ed Mohr (and his laughing song); Charlie, Bob, and Art Moore (who could spit tobacco through the eye of needle at five paces); Bill Walters (who had stories that were almost unbelievable); Bill Kerr (who was always willing to use his pick-up for the purpose of taking young people to dances); Tom Louther (who was always telling us about the argument between the devil and the Lord); the Burt family (who gave us such great hospitality and had memories like elephants); Jock Morrison (who chinked his cabin, on the inside, with cow manure); and the Indian we called Old Sam (who served Dad and I lynx stew cooked with head, eyeballs, and all.

Furthermore, I shall always remember Oscar Johnson and Reuben Nelson, who had the store at Ootsa Lake when I was a child; they always gave us a bag of candy when we bought groceries. Then there was an old friend of Dad's, Ted Lewis, who -- when he came to visit -- would always ask: "Al, how's your tobacco?" After I passed him the can in response, and he would roll a dozen cigarettes, saying over and over: "To hell with the expense."

Of course, there are others, most of them long departed from this earth. Indeed, another chapter in our lives ended last year when Marion's sister Beatrice passed away after an eighteen-month fight with cancer. Bea was a great organizer and loved to dance. We were part of a folk and square dance group for many years. She was also social director of the local Sons of Norway lodge, and (if the truth be known) its strength. I have been president of the lodge for the past two years, and saw declining interest in it since the onset of Bea's illness. (In case you're wondering, Marion's parents were both Scandinavian. Although mine were English, I am told that I am Scandinavian by contamination.)

This year brought more sorrow. On January 21, 1998, my brother Stan passed away. His ashes will be spread over Blackwell Hill, that rocky bluff I used to climb when young just for a glimpse of Ootsa Lake and the mountains beyond. It's located on the original property Dad staked in 1910; Stan spent nearly seventy years on the land, and raised his family there. Later, a plaque will be set in the rock of Blackwell Hill in memory of my brother, born April 9, 1928.

Yet despite these sad events, the future is not bleak. As Marion and I continue our life here on Ootsa Lake, we can only hope and pray that good health stays with us, because we plan to live here as long as we are physically able. We do not know what the future holds, but I sincerely hope neither of us will ever be confined to a hospital bed.

I dedicate this history of my life to my family and friends, and hope they enjoy reading it as much as I did writing it. I also hope that in the future, many people will visit this area and beautiful Tweedsmuir Park, which -- as the title of this book indicates -- is truly paradise.

Sand Cabin Bay, Eutsuk Lake.

Whitesail Lake.

BIBLIOGRAPHY

I have used the following works as references for this book. Many thanks to their authors and publishers.

Burns Lake and District:
A History Formal and Informal, by Pat Turkki.
Heritage Lost, by Jean Clark Giesbrecht.
History of the First Special Service Force, by Lt. Col. Robert Burhans.
A Commemorative History of the First Special Service Force, by the First Special Service Force Association.
From Snowshoes to Politics, by Cyril Shelford.

At this time, I also wish to thank my wife Marion, Cyril Shelford, Michael Turkki, and June Moulton for their assistance in completing this autobiography, as well as my many relatives and friends for all their encouragement.